Making a Collection Count

CHANDOS

INFORMATION PROFESSIONAL SERIES

Series Editor: Ruth Rikowski
(Email: Rikowskigr@aol.com)

Chandos' new series of books is aimed at the busy information professional. They have been specially commissioned to provide the reader with an authoritative view of current thinking. They are designed to provide easy-to-read and (most importantly) practical coverage of topics that are of interest to librarians and other information professionals. If you would like a full listing of current and forthcoming titles, please visit our website, *www. chandospublishing.com*, email *wp@woodheadpublishing*.com or telephone +44 (0) 1223 499140.

New authors: we are always pleased to receive ideas for new titles; if you would like to write a book for Chandos, please contact Dr Glyn Jones on *gjones@chandospublishing.com* or telephone +44 (0) 1993 848726.

Bulk orders: some organisations buy a number of copies of our books. If you are interested in doing this, we would be pleased to discuss a discount. Please email *wp@woodheadpublishing.com* or telephone +44 (0) 1223 499140.

Making a Collection Count

A holistic approach to library collection management

Second edition

HOLLY HIBNER AND MARY KELLY

Oxford Cambridge New Delhi

Chandos Publishing
Hexagon House
Avenue 4
Station Lane
Witney
Oxford OX28 4BN
UK
Tel: +44(0) 1993 848726
Email: *info@chandospublishing.com*
www.chandospublishing.com
www.chandospublishingonline.com

Chandos Publishing is an imprint of Woodhead Publishing Limited

Woodhead Publishing Limited
80 High Street
Sawston
Cambridge CB22 3HJ
UK
Tel: +44(0) 1223 499140
Fax: +44(0) 1223 832819
www.woodheadpublishing.com

First published in 2013

ISBN: 978-1-84334-760-6 (print)

ISBN: 978-1-78063-441-8 (online)

Chandos Information Professional Series ISSN: 2052-210X (print) and
ISSN: 2052-2118 (online)

Library of Congress Control Number: 2013948267

British Library Cataloguing-in-Publication Data.
A catalogue record for this book is available from the British Library.

The publisher makes no representation, express or implied, with regard to the accuracy of the information contained in this publication and cannot accept any legal responsibility or liability for any errors or omissions.

The material contained in this publication constitutes general guidelines only and does not represent to be advice on any particular matter. No reader or purchaser should act on the basis of material contained in this publication without first taking professional advice appropriate to their particular circumstances. All screenshots in this publication are the copyright of the website owner(s), unless indicated otherwise.

Typeset by RefineCatch Limited, Bungay, Suffolk

Contents

Contents

Contents

List of figures

About the authors

Holly Hibner is the Adult Services Coordinator at the Plymouth District Library in Plymouth, MI. She received an MLIS degree from Wayne State University in 1999. Since that time, she has published and spoken on a variety of topics, and received the 2007 Loleta Fyan award from the Michigan Library Association for innovation in library service.

Mary Kelly is the Youth Services Librarian at the Lyon Township Public Library in South Lyon, MI. She received both an MBA and an MLIS from Wayne State University. Mary has published and presented on topics such as collection quality, computer instruction, reader's advisory, and providing tech support.

Together, Mary and Holly created the popular blog "Awful Library Books" (*www.awfullibrarybooks.net*).

Acknowledgments

We wish to thank the many libraries and librarians throughout our local area for allowing us access to their history, collections, facilities, technology, and staff. We would particularly like to thank the Plymouth District Library in Plymouth, Michigan and the Lyon Township Public Library in South Lyon, Michigan for their cooperation. Many thanks to our colleagues for inspiration and to our families for encouragement.

Acknowledgments

We wish to thank the many libraries and librarians throughout our local area for allowing us access to their history, collections, facilities, technology, and staff. We would particularly like to thank the Plymouth District Library in Plymouth, Michigan and the Lyon Township Public Library in South Lyon, Michigan for their cooperation. Many thanks to our colleagues for inspiration, and to our families for encouragement.

Introduction

After many years of working on improving library service, we realized that we needed to revise our methodology. We were trying to improve one thing at a time, but the truth is that the library is a single entity of many services that are completely integrated – almost symbiotic. Everything we do stems from making information available for someone to use. Every other activity comes from that singular purpose. In order to provide the best possible library service, we need to understand the ties between various library functions.

We started looking at library service holistically, taking into account how each piece functions relative to the whole institution. This book focuses on how these relationships affect library collection quality. We need to look at our collections with fresh eyes regularly. We need to ask ourselves if the information we provide is relevant for our users, or if the community's needs and tastes have changed. We especially need to keep an eye on economic trends that cause us to change the collection's scope and focus. The library collection is an evolving entity within a library, changing and growing with the times and creating an eclectic mix of items. To bring library collections back into focus, they need to be actively managed.

As our approach to improving and updating our collections became more holistic, we realized that we had been fixing the obvious problems without addressing the multitude of their origins. Changing one thing had a snowball effect on various related areas of the library, effectively causing more problems. We defined what we call the life cycle of the collection, and tried to take each step of the cycle into consideration when making future improvements. We tried to trace problems to their origins, even when that took us out of our own departments, budgets, and comfort zones.

This book is divided into nine chapters, and attempts to apply general collection management principles to achieving collection quality. In the beginning, we will talk about our collection life cycle model, which is the basis for a holistic library environment. Understanding what happens at each stage of a collection's life cycle is the key to making globally acceptable decisions for a library.

Chapter 2 is a unique portion of this book. We learn to evaluate the processes and procedures that a library's staff follows in order to carry out their work. Careful documentation and analysis of a library's workflows are an important aspect of quality control because they create channels for communication, deeper understanding of library work outside of one's own work space, and greater efficiency and accuracy. This chapter reminds all of us that a collection doesn't exist in a vacuum; actual people interact with it constantly.

Chapters 3, 4, and 5 received the bulk of the revisions and edits for the second edition of this book. They were completely re-organized and two new chapters were created. We wanted to expand the information on gathering, reporting, and using data to support collection decision-making. We have separated the data gathering (chapter 3: using metrics to measure the collection and performing a collection audit) from the data reporting (chapter 4: performing physical inventory to ensure accuracy of the data presented in ILS reports) and the data analysis (chapter 5: using statistics to analyze collection performance).

Chapter 3 shows how an integrated library system (ILS, sometimes referred to as an automation system) can be mined for a wealth of data. Here we focus on metrics, or ways we can measure the collection and its use. This chapter also describes how to audit a collection to see if there is an error rate among the catalog records that indicates a larger problem. This goes hand-in-hand with the workflow analysis suggested in chapter 2. If a library's workflows are efficient, a collection audit should reveal that the collections are properly indicated in the catalog. A breakdown in either the workflow or collection performance could lead to a need for more in-depth study.

That in-depth study is described in chapter 4. Performing a physical inventory is suggested as a way to find and fix errors hinted at by the workflow analysis and collection audit. A physical inventory puts the collection in the hands of the analysts, item by item. Once an initial inventory is completed and corrections are made, physical inventory can become part of ongoing collection management.

Once the collection is measured and audited (chapter 3), and inventoried (chapter 4), statistics can be created and collection performance can be analyzed. Collection use, average age, and turnover rates are discussed in this chapter. Prioritizing and making difficult decisions with respect to specific materials and resource allocation can be achieved more easily with this kind of supporting data.

Chapter 6 discusses collection objectives and benchmarks. Along with physical inventory and statistics, collection objectives and benchmarks allow systematic evaluation of a collection's performance. Libraries can improve service and reduce costs and waste. They will be able to respond quickly to changing circumstances, such as budget cuts and curriculum changes. The integrated library system (ILS) is put to use again to provide data for this evaluation. Collection objectives and benchmarks are another approach to ongoing collection management.

Chapter 7 takes a look at a library's physical spaces. The layout of a building and of individual collections impacts their use, as well as their value. Here we discuss the use of classification systems, signage, and displays to impact the quality of a collection. A change in any of these areas affects other stages of the collection's life cycle.

Chapter 8 presents everyone's bottom line: the library's budget. Advice is given for many ways to get the most out of a collection budget. Readers are invited to be innovative and consider all of the resources available to us. Since everything we do stems from making information available for someone to use, we need to find alternative ways of procuring that information. Negotiating with vendors, resource sharing between libraries, and collection philosophy are all included in chapter 8.

Our final chapter sums up the idea of holistic library environments. Everything is connected. All library services play into each other, sometimes in invisible ways. Four specific library resources are emphasized in this chapter, and the connections between them are described: staff, collection, facility, and technology. Library budgets are described from yet another angle here, as well as library programming.

We understand that collection quality-audits and large-scale updating and correcting of library collections can seem overwhelming. After all, even small libraries have thousands of items. This book recommends a manageable process whereby smaller pieces of the whole collection are dealt with at a time.

Many generations of librarians have left their mark on a library's collection from their efforts. We wish to progress that tradition by expanding the care used in collection management and a holistic approach to library service. It is our hope that the ideas presented in this book will translate into a meaningful improvement in any library setting, regardless of size, type, or mission.

Life cycle of a collection

Abstract: The library's collection is a constantly changing entity. Various library departments, staff and users interact with the collection. This chapter describes the eight stages of the collection life cycle. Each stage is an opportunity to survey the collection and monitor for quality. The eight stages are: selection, acquisitions, processing and cataloging, shelving, checkout (use), re-shelving, repair/maintenance, and weed or replace.

Key words: collection life cycle, collection development, collection management, e-books, self-published, weeding, book sales, storage, archive, floating collections.

Some time ago, a colleague was asked by a library board member when the staff would be "done" buying books for the library. He was under the impression that the library added materials until the shelves were full, and then they were finished. The truth is that library collections have a life cycle that is never finished. Various departments, as well as the public, interact with the collection in different ways, each contributing to its quality. As you can see in the diagram overleaf, there are eight stages in the collection life cycle. Each stage is an opportunity to survey the collection and evaluate it for quality. This chapter will describe the stages of the life cycle in detail, and how they relate to each other in holistic collection management. (See Figure 1.1.)

Collection life cycle

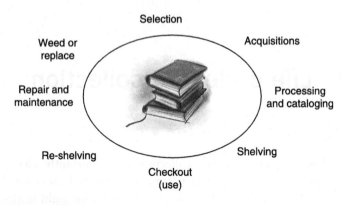

Selection

Weed or
replace

Acquisitions

Repair and
maintenance

Processing
and cataloging

Re-shelving

Shelving

Checkout
(use)

Figure 1.1   Collection life cycle

Collection management policies

Having a good collection management policy is the foundation of a quality collection. All collection decisions are driven by this policy. We've emphasized the word "management," rather than calling it a "collection development policy" or a "materials selection policy" so that the entire life cycle of a collection is represented in the policy. Developing a collection is a small part of the life cycle. The word "development" implies growth, which points to the selection piece of the life cycle, while the word "management" implies control and attention. A good collection management policy helps staff make decisions that affect the entire collection life cycle. The American Library Association calls them "collection policy statements" and defines them as statements which "serve as public planning, allocation, informational, administrative, and training documents. They further the systematic, rational, appropriate, and timely selection, de-selection, and preservation of materials" (Anderson, 1996, p.1). This is a nice, broad phrase that represents all aspects of collection management, and works well with our holistic view of collection management too.

In order to be truly useful, a collection management policy needs to be updated regularly – perhaps annually. Formats change, and even the library's collection philosophy or mission can change from year to year. For example, during the recent economic crisis in the U.S., many public libraries needed to focus their collection goals on career and personal finance information. Any global situation, such as a war, can impact the way a collection is managed in any given year. Perhaps donations will be more aggressively sought or accepted to lessen the impact of a lowered collection budget. Perhaps more money is necessary for a particular subject area or format. Each year, the library's collection management policy should be re-examined. New goals and objectives should be written. Rose Anjejo points out, in an article titled "Collection Development Policies for Small Libraries," that once a library completes the basic work and writes a policy, updating it is not a "monumental problem" (2006, p.13). Only the specifics for the upcoming year need to be addressed. This is true in any size or type of library.

A literature review reveals some disagreement between libraries about whether individual collections and formats should be addressed separately in collection management policies. One study described a 2004 survey where "fewer than half of the respondents indicated that their institution has a collection development policy specifically for the audiovisual collection" (Bergman and Laskowski, 2004, p.91). On the other side, Anjejo advocates for the use of a collection development policy "particularly with regard to electronic resources" (2006, p.13). Of course, procedures specific to a library, as well as organization of a collection management team will determine what is included in a library's policy. For example, if a library separates non-fiction DVDs from feature films in terms of budget, selectors, or shelving, these are considerations for writing a collection management policy for each collection. Other examples of divisions in collections and formats could be reference and non-fiction, "popular" audio books and language instruction audios, test preparation materials and general non-fiction, or career materials and general non-fiction. When libraries decide to separate these otherwise similar materials, they have already decided that they are unique to their library and their users in some way. The collection management policy should point out the reasons why they have been separated, what makes them different in terms of selection, purchasing, processing, use, maintenance, and what the criteria will be for weeding them.

Collection management policies should also take digital materials into consideration, as those materials need to be managed throughout their life cycle as well. Of course, not all stages of the life cycle apply to e-books. For example, shelving does not affect digital collections. As we go through the stages of the life cycle, digital materials will be considered.

See Appendix A: Sample collection management policy for a public library.

Selection

At the top of the collection life cycle is selection. Materials are carefully chosen for library collections from a sea of available titles. Selectors must decide which materials best match their library's mission and policies, and stick to a budget.

Libraries of all types often assign specific selectors to specific collections. In this arrangement, one person makes the final selections for their assigned collections. This gives selectors a sense of ownership of a collection and encourages deep understanding and familiarity with their assigned areas. It is important to put a person in charge of each collection who can oversee its management and make executive decisions. A managed collection is one that is watched, worked with, and understood.

That said, there are also benefits to staff collaboration in selection. When there is only one person making decisions for a collection, it can become stagnant; a reflection of one person's philosophy, interests, and opinions. By assigning collaborators, a wider viewpoint is reflected in the collection. Perhaps a collection leader can make final selection decisions, but that person has the help of collaborators. Even those not assigned to the selection team can make suggestions for any collection, further broadening the perspective of those interested in – and those using – the materials.

Consider an academic library where a selector gains input from faculty who are specialists in the field, students who are using the materials, and fellow library staff who may have a background in the subject area. These three points of view would result in a cutting-edge, varied perspective toward the selection of the collection. An example of this is the University of Botswana Library. Their collection team is "a coordinated effort between subject librarians and the Faculties. Users are also invited to suggest titles to be ordered" (Fombad and Mutula, 2003, p.69). In a public library, a collection management team can share review sources, passing review journals around the office and through departments. Since everyone has access to the same reviews, they can all comment on the same titles, formats, and subjects. Everyone has a stake in the final collection in a public library, where staff members are more likely to share reference responsibilities. A public library with a popular materials collection may have a team of reference staff who help the general public use all library materials in all subject areas and across formats. They all need to be aware of what is in the collection. Having the ability to suggest additions to the collection in areas where they have found holes is helpful to everyone who uses it. In fact, allowing library users in any kind of library to make suggestions to selectors can only help to round out the collection.

Not only does collaboration help library users and staff become aware of the collections managed by others, but it also helps selectors of different formats avoid duplication – or duplicate where most appropriate. In difficult economic times, or anywhere a strict budget must be adhered to, redundancy is a burden. Selectors can help each other by choosing which formats they need, and rely on each other to fill in gaps that individual budgets cannot fill. In a public library, selectors may choose to purchase a particular title in large print, regular print, and audio format, but not add it to their e-book collection. In an academic library, the choice may be made to purchase a serial in electronic format but not in print.

Knowing what is being selected across departments helps library staff market collections, too. A public library may have collections specifically for children, teens, adults, and seniors, but those collections may include titles of interest across the spectrum. Public libraries chart their success partially by usage statistics, so whenever staff cross-market collections they help the library as a whole. This holistic library service makes library patrons aware of other parts of the library that they might not have used otherwise. In an academic library, there are similar implications for cross-curricular marketing. Items selected by the staff member in charge of one discipline may be of use to library patrons in another subject area. Collaborating on selection of materials for various fields of study in a college library saves the selectors time and money, but also educates them – and their patrons – on how various subject areas are related.

Selecting for digital collections has become more complicated over the years. The technology has come a long way: databases often have mobile-friendly access and e-books are increasingly available across platforms. Just as digital materials become more accessible, though, selecting and managing them for library users has become more difficult. Publishers have created restrictions, manufacturers of specific mobile devices have adopted proprietary file formats, and the delivery systems that authorize users by library cards or student IDs have become more layered and complicated. A discussion of these obstacles and how different libraries are handling them can be found in Paula Hane's article, "A Librarian e-book Revolution?" (2012, p.10). She notes that some librarians are deciding to develop their own e-book collections, such as the Douglas County (Colorado) Libraries where staff developed software to deliver e-books to their members directly, working with publishers to purchase e-books and deliver them in a way that is mutually beneficial to writers, publishers, and library users (p.10).

Libraries are also encouraged to include a statement in their collection management policy about selecting self-published and print-on-demand titles. The University of the South Pacific Library created a useful LibGuide about vanity presses that indicates that the quality of self-published materials can be low because the companies that print self-published materials will often print anything, regardless of the merit or reputation of the author or the sales potential of the title (Phillips, 2013). They are also careful to note that "some notable and successful novels began as self-published works" and that their list of print-on-demand publishers does not guarantee poor quality by those companies (Phillips, 2013). Print-on-demand and vanity presses are rising in popularity, though, and libraries will want to decide whether these materials are a good match for their collection goals.

Purchasing/acquisitions

Once items are selected, they are purchased. This is the stage in the collection life cycle where libraries interact with outside vendors. Purchasers need to shop vendors for the best deals on shipping, delivery, and ease of ordering. They will want to consider which vendors offer replacements of items like cases or discs that come up missing or damaged later on. Items need to be able to be fixed, replaced, and re-ordered quickly and easily. Purchasers should know where to get the best quality items that will last a long time, arrive quickly, and ship and invoice efficiently.

When selectors choose small press titles, acquisitions staff may have more difficulty procuring them. Jeff Lilburn, author of "Re-examining the Concept of Neutrality for Academic Libraries," says, "it would appear that small and independent publishers are, and will continue to be, critical in the building of broad and balanced collections that more accurately reflect the diversity of ideas" (2003, p.31). These titles may be important in libraries that try to present a balanced collection, but can be difficult to get a hold of. They have smaller print runs and are often not available through major wholesalers. Purchasers need to be aware of alternative methods of obtaining these items.

It is helpful if the acquisitions department is included in the collection management policy. The policy can list the vendors the library uses regularly, criteria for purchasing from a new vendor, what costs the library is willing to pay (such as shipping or service fees), return policies, the number of copies a library will buy or criteria for purchasing additional copies, and the use of purchase orders, credit, cash, and staff reimbursement for library materials. It could also include whether or not the library is willing to consider adding used materials to its collections, either from sites like *amazon.com*, *alibris.com*, or *ebay.com* or from in-person donations of materials to the library.

Another way to ensure a quality collection at the acquisitions stage of the collection life cycle, as well as ensuring a lean workflow, is for purchasers to place orders for library materials on a schedule that works across departments. Regular orders can be staggered so that technical services staff can keep up with the work coming in. Communication between departments is key. For example, if a youth department in a public library needs a particular item to arrive in time to present a special program, purchasers need to know that. Or, if several copies of a particular title are needed for a class, the faculty needs to make that known to a college library's purchasers.

Timing is also important in regards to the relevancy and currency of the items being purchased. When a selector chooses an item for a collection, they expect the item to be available to library users in a timely fashion. If the acquisitions department does not place the order, the technical services staff do not prepare the item for circulation, and the shelvers do not get the item onto the shelves, it may become irrelevant before library users ever have access to it. In public libraries, national bestsellers need to be made available to the public quickly, while they are still popular and in demand. In special libraries in fields like law or medicine, currency is absolutely crucial – even life-altering! New materials have to be made available to library users as quickly as possible in order to stay relevant and current.

Purchasing digital content usually requires a contract. Someone will need to have the authority to sign these agreements, which often deal with remote access, the expiration date of the service, and large amounts of money (some databases cost tens of thousands of dollars or more!). Again, cross-departmental communication is crucial. Selectors may only want a certain portion of a database or a certain format of e-book, which purchasers need to know when setting up contracts. IT departments may get involved to set up modes of authenticating users remotely for access to the digital materials. All parties should understand whether the library owns digital content or simply leases access to content owned by the vendor.

Processing and cataloging

For the purposes of this discussion, we define "processing" as the fixation of labels, bar codes, covers, cases, and other physical pieces that make an item ready for library shelves. Processing and cataloging have been lumped together in our life cycle model because they directly relate to each other. The labels placed on an item need to reflect exactly what is in the catalog record so that when an item is found through a catalog search, library users will know what to look for at the shelf – and on which shelf to look. Processing and cataloging are often handled by the same department: technical services.

It is important to have processing and cataloging manuals or checklists to ensure that items are processed and cataloged consistently. Having all items in a collection look similar makes them easier for library users to find what they want. It also makes the items easier for staff to shelve. For example, a public library could have a mystery book collection that all include a mystery genre sticker on the spine. An academic library could have a documentary DVD collection where each item is labeled as such with a special sticker. Similarly, all mystery books should be cataloged with a consistent call number scheme, such as the word "Mystery" and the author's last name (see Figure 2.1). This makes a shelf list print nicer, which will come into play when running reports and taking collection inventory.

Processing rules set by an institution need to make sense for each collection. The prescribed sticker placement should make items easier to use, so they should not cover important information like the title or author's name. When someone looks up a title in the online catalog, and then goes to the library shelf to find it, having a variety of stickers covering

Figure 1.2 A mystery collection

important information would make the item very difficult to locate. Processing should help, not hinder, use of a collection. Some things to consider include:

- Do cases have locks that are easy to set or open?
- Are spine labels printed in a font size that most people can see?
- Do the words on the spine labels make sense?
- Do they match the words in the item's catalog record?
- Are there plastic covers and tape on the items to protect them?
- How about labels that identify the owning library and bar code numbers on various parts?

These are all questions that need to be answered to make the items in the collection the most useful and those that last the longest.

Cataloging rules also need to make sense for each collection, and even for each library. Public libraries sometimes take more creative license with the Dewey Decimal System, making certain materials easier to find. For example, at the Plymouth District Library in Plymouth, MI, the youth department has decided to catalog non-fiction animal books by the animal name rather than by the author's last name. In that library, books about dolphins can be found all together under the call number 599.5 DOLPHIN. Books about tigers are under 599.75 TIGER. They have decided that this makes all books on one particular animal easier for children to find. The same library also re-cataloged Shakespeare plays under the title of the play rather than all of them scattered under the traditional call number of 822.33 SHAKESPEARE. Rather, one can find all available editions of *Romeo and Juliet* under 822.33 ROMEO, *Macbeth* under 822.33 MACBETH, *Othello* under 822.33 OTHELLO, etc. This cuts the time it takes a patron to find a specific play significantly shorter than when they had to peruse all of the 822.33 SHAKESPEARE call numbers for the one they want. It also makes these items faster and easier for shelvers to re-shelve.

Libraries should consider cataloging their digital collections if their ILS (integrated library system) allows it. Patrons who are unaware that the library subscribes to a third-party e-book catalog will benefit from finding records in the library catalog for those digital titles when they search. Catalogs with integrated, or federated, searching features may even be able to link to specific journal articles in the library's databases. Everything searchable – and therefore findable – depends on its cataloging, so it is an extremely important piece of the collection life cycle.

Shelving

Once items are processed and cataloged, they are ready to be shelved. Shelving implications for a quality collection include accuracy, shelf space, size, and timing.

Accuracy in shelving is crucial. When the library catalog points users to a particular section to find an item, users expect to find the item there. Mis-shelved items cause frustration on the part of library staff and patrons. "Shelf reading" is an important activity that library shelvers usually undertake. They go through the items one at a time, putting them back in order.

Shelf space is an ongoing struggle for many libraries. In order to add something new, they may have to take something away. Knowing how many items exist in a collection and what percentage of those items is checked out at any given time can help manage shelf space. Refer to the sections in this book on physical inventory and shelf balancing for further discussion. For this discussion of the collection life cycle, we can say that a quality collection is one in which every item has a comfortable space on the shelf when it is ready to be put away.

Size of items to be shelved is another consideration when managing a collection. Libraries may need to create an "oversized item" collection so that they can be put in a place where shelf space is appropriate to large items. D. Yvonne Jones's article "Oversized and Underused" discusses how the placement of oversized items in academic libraries affects their circulation (2006). Of the libraries surveyed, 47 percent shelved oversized items in a completely separate area from the general circulating material with the same classification. A smaller number of libraries shelved oversized materials closer to the general circulating material, such as on the same floor. Ultimately, an examination of circulation data showed "no apparent difference in circulation based on the shelving strategy used" (Jones, 2006, p.331). While moving oversized items out of the general collection may not affect their circulation, it does extend the life of the items when they can be shelved comfortably(see Figures 1.3 and 1.4). Putting them sideways on regular shelves causes them to stick out into the aisles. People and carts run into them, knocking them to the floor, breaking their spines, bending pages, and causing other physical damage.

The reverse, very small books, pose their own problems. Tiny books tend to get lost on the shelves. They can fall behind the shelves easily. They can also get misplaced by patrons who check them out, putting them at high risk for circulation issues.

Size also contributes to processing: big books require larger cover protector sheets and large items like CD-ROMs or audio books with many discs may require larger cases

Figure 1.3 Oversized books interfiled with other books, sticking out into the aisles, are a hazard for shelving carts!

Figure 1.4 Oversized books lying sideways in specially-sized shelves in separate areas of the library collection

(and, conversely, small items require special processing materials too). Having these processing materials on hand is necessary to being able to process odd-sized items consistently and correctly. Some collections are predisposed to large sizes, such as maps and art books. Libraries with these collections need to take care to shelve these items suitably.

Timing, in terms of shelving, can be a tricky situation. The number of items ready to be shelved could go from minimal to extreme depending on various factors. For example, if a library closes for a holiday, they may return to an overflowing book return. All of those items will need to be shelved at once. Where does the library store items ready to be re-shelved? Is there ample space for them? An academic library may see an influx of returns at the end of a semester when students are finished writing papers and have completed their final exams. Will there be time to re-shelve them before the next semester begins? Another aspect of timing has to do with purchasing. If various staff members select for their collections all at once, the purchasers, processors, and catalogers will be inundated with materials to work on, and therefore lots of items will become ready to shelve all at once. In any library, a purchasing schedule will help keep an even flow of materials to process and shelve. A well-managed collection is one that makes its way to the shelf as quickly as possible so that patrons can use the items.

A simple form (as in Figure 1.5) can be attached to carts of materials waiting to be shelved to give staff an idea of what is on the cart and how long it has been waiting to be shelved. It is a good technique for tracking and managing shelving issues, especially in large libraries. This technique can be used to determine where in the shelving process that leaning is most needed.

Shelving Cart Form

Collection _____

Date cart created _____

Date cart shelved _____

Time shelving started _____ Time shelving finished _____

Shelver's initials _____

Figure 1.5 Shelving cart form

Use

Once the collection is on the shelf, it is ready for library patrons. "Use" includes browsing at the shelf and check-out. The point of a library collection is to make information available to library users, so a quality collection is one that library patrons actually use.

The check-out procedure is also part of use. At check-out, the final decision on use is made. Can reference books be checked out? Are all parts of the item present? Are they in working order? The answers to these questions determine the patron's ability to use the item. This is a great place in the life cycle of the item to take stock of its usefulness.

The check-out phase is one where a familiarity with various modules of the library's ILS (integrated library system) will be helpful. For example, an understanding of what happens to an item record in cataloging could be very useful to the circulation department. If an item was mistakenly cataloged as a reference book, it would explain why a patron is having trouble checking it out. It may not be obvious by looking at the item itself, which would not have the labels of other reference books, so the ability to look more closely at an item record and recognize an error – and be able to fix it – will lean the check-out process considerably. Reference librarians trying to place holds for patrons may need access to the patron's circulation record to see if there are fines or expired records they can deal with. Being able to work with item and patron records outside of one's specific departmental role in these examples encourages the ultimate goal: use of the item. It also encourages holistic collection management across departments since everyone can improve catalog records and ensure positive patron experiences.

There are also quality considerations for the use of digital collections. For example, libraries with public access computers should try to make digital collections accessible on those terminals. If special software, plug-ins, or peripherals are required, the library should consider making them available for patron use. Something else to consider is whether digital materials are available for simultaneous use by multiple patrons at once, or if a system of requests and holds is in place if it is a one-user model.

Repair and maintenance

Use creates wear and tear and ages library materials. This is a normal part of the collection life cycle, of course, so repair of damaged items needs to be acknowledged. A quality collection is one that works; that is not broken or torn or missing pieces or pages.

Frank Hoffmann and Richard Wood, authors of *Library Collection Development Policies*, suggest that collection maintenance be included in a collection development policy (2005). Their definition of maintenance includes "binding, disaster preparedness, preservation, replacement, and weeding," and they make a good point that there is a "renewed emphasis on protecting library resources in the face of exploding costs for both new technology and traditional materials" (Hoffmann and Wood, 2005, p.181). Their idea of including disaster preparedness in a collection management policy is also important. Recent natural disasters had impacts on library collections that we can all learn from and prepare better for in the future, like the 2011 Japanese tsunami and Hurricane Sandy on the east coast of the U.S. in Fall of 2012.

Many libraries have a special area dedicated to items that need mending. It is important to temporarily re-catalog those items as "damaged" or "mending" – or whatever term the library's ILS uses for this situation – so that their status no longer makes the item seem available to patrons who look it up in the catalog. It is also important that those items actually get repaired! This is a wonderful job for volunteers or student help. They can buff out scratches in discs and repair book bindings easily. Having a schedule for repair work may help staff prioritize getting those items back in circulation.

Check-in

This is the point where the life cycle repeats. A quality collection is partially determined by what is returned. If items go out, but don't come back in, they are obviously no longer useful. Check-in is another point in the life cycle where staff can make sure all parts and pieces are accounted for, as well as the item's condition.

Libraries of all types have used special promotions like "amnesty days" and even collection agencies to try to get long-overdue items back to the library. The important thing to consider is that the life cycle of an item is interrupted when it is in a limbo-status like "long-overdue" or "lost." At some point, a library must cut its losses and decide how long an item is to remain in limbo in the catalog before it is removed from the system (whether they have received the item back or not). A long list of long-overdues does nothing to help get the items back, receive payment for those items, or to keep the catalog clean. Collection management policies should include a statement of how long item records are kept in the system with these "limbo" statuses before the library gives up and moves on. Of course, *some* time should pass and efforts be made to recover those items, but they can't stay lost forever.

In a perfect scenario, an item is returned and checked back in, and can be re-shelved. The life cycle repeats!

Weeding

At the end of the life cycle is de-selection, or weeding. Once an item no longer meets the needs of the library's users, or no longer matches the library's mission, it should be removed from the collection. A quality collection is highly dependent upon weeding to remove items that are bringing the collection down.

Some would argue that falling budgets to replace old items, as well as smaller staffs to perform the task make weeding difficult. They would say it is better to have old items on the shelf than to weed them and have very little for users to choose from. Chris Jones, author of "Maintaining a Healthy Library Collection: the Need to Weed" would disagree (2007). Jones analyzed statistics gathered in public libraries in New South Wales, Australia that showed that "the age of library resources is a major factor in their usage" (2007, p.170). In the end, the libraries with the freshest collections in terms of publication dates had higher circulations than those with bigger collections with an older average age. It is better to weed an old collection so that it has fewer, but more current, items. A quality collection is not determined by size, but by the items that make up the collection. Anne Felix of the Grand Prairie (Texas) Public Library System said it best: "A good library is like a good haircut. It's not what you cut – it's what you leave" (Larson, 2008, p.5).

What do libraries with well-maintained collections do with items they weed? Many public libraries hold used book sales where they sell some of their weeded items. Another option is what Munroe, Haar, and Johnson call "transfer programs" in their book *Guide to Collection Development and Management Administration, Organization, and Staffing* (2001). They say that "transfer is the relocation of materials to another branch or to a closed-stack storage facility" (Munroe, Haar, and Johnson, 2001, p.4). Items weeded from one collection might be transferred to storage or another branch. They could also be transferred to a museum, archive, or a special collection in another library or organization. When weeding the last holding in a library cooperative, some libraries can send it to their state library, if the state library serves as a depository for last copies in this manner.

Transfer programs are similar to the idea of floating collections. Floating collections "remain where patrons return them, rather than being shipped to an owning branch" (Johal and Quigley, 2012, p.13). Floating collections have implications for every stage in the collection life cycle, since they may start in one location and end in another building entirely. Standards across library branches are crucial to the success of floating collections. Rather than weed an item entirely, it could be sent to a branch library where it may be better used. This avoids what Johal and Quigley call "crisis weeding" (2012, p.14). This is where one branch weeds materials to make space in their facility, when those materials could be used in another branch. Floating collections, when managed carefully, balance the collection to the locations where they are most-used.

A wonderful article by Caryl Gray and Paul Metz entitled "Public Relations and Library Weeding" points out that weeding can be a public relations matter (2005). They suggest that any large weeding project begin with publicity that invites discussion and comment from the library's stakeholders. When Virginia Tech University Libraries discarded over 160,000 volumes and transferred another 270,000 volumes to storage between 1995 and 2002, they laid the groundwork with the faculty and kept them in the loop throughout the process. They believe this avoided "ill will and suspicion" and kept faculty from the idea that librarians were "conspiring to send 'their' books away" (Metz and Gray, 2005, p.274). In addition to advance publicity, Virginia Tech followed a weeding policy, were flexible about items that faculty found important enough to keep or return from storage, gave some items to correctional facilities, the English Department, libraries around the U.S. and other countries, and made every effort to recycle rather than send them to the landfill. These good deeds helped their large weeding project to be successful and to gain the buy-in of library users.

Those who manage library collections in any format should keep their library's mission and collection management policy in mind at all stages of the collection life cycle. If the library is not an archive, and does not have a mission to store or preserve materials indefinitely, weeding is a necessary step to keep the collection fresh. Non-archival libraries generally collect and provide access to information – they don't collect books for the sake of having books on the shelf. Books are physical items, which museums and archives may be interested in collecting. Other libraries, such as publics and academics, need to distance themselves from the medium and focus on the content. If the information contained in the item is no longer useful, or if access to that information has become difficult, the item needs to be weeded.

Following this logic, digital collections must also be weeded. They don't take up any shelf space (though they might take up digital storage space) and physical condition will never be a factor, so it is especially important that digital collection managers focus on the information they contain. Alice Crosetto's article "Weeding E-books" says, "When libraries began acquiring nonprint resources, policies that were drafted to reflect the new formats did not alter the libraries' missions, nor did they eliminate the concept of evaluating collections and withdrawing items." (Crosetto, 2011). The article points out that usage statistics are usually available for digital platforms, which can be used to help staff decide which titles to weed. Crosetto also points out that some vendors allow weeded e-books to be archived by the library, while others may remove access completely or not allow weeding at all (Crosetto, 2011). Publication dates and formats should also be considered. For example, if a library has a collection of reference books on CD-ROMs, but no computers with CD-ROM drives, the collection is a strong candidate for weeding. Perhaps those same CD-ROMs require software that is incompatible with upgraded operating systems. Again, they should be strongly considered for weeding.

Conclusion

Each stage of the collection life cycle presents opportunities to evaluate and improve its quality. We have described various techniques for managing collections at each stage of the life cycle and suggested ways to gather information about a collection's status. Managing collections holistically takes each stage of the collection life cycle into consideration when making decisions, and recognizes that each stage of the life cycle has implications for the others.

Understanding your workflow

Abstract: Workflow analysis provides a deeper understanding of the processes laid out in the collection life cycle. Dissecting the functions of multiple departments and employees illuminate inefficiencies and create a quality check on library processes. A thorough understanding of a library's processes can save resources and improve efficiency.

Key words: workflow analysis, lean, efficiency, streamlining, ergonomics, quality assurance, selection, purchase orders, RFID, collection life cycle.

Tracking the flow of materials through the library system can guide staff to possible checkpoints of quality. In the previous chapter, we discussed how the collection has a life cycle. In order to properly and fully manage a collection, it is essential to understand exactly what happens at each stage of the life cycle. This can be done through an examination of workflows. A workflow is how things are done, by whom, and when. Analyzing a workflow requires a thorough understanding of the system. A workflow analysis is a complete documentation of the sequence of steps within a given process. This chapter details a sample workflow at each stage of the life cycle. Emphasis will be placed on ways to lean workflows for maximum efficiency.

The analysis of each workflow can be an illuminating exercise for the staff and managers of a library. Most people would probably be surprised at the actual process of what happens where and when. Diagramming and analyzing workflows throughout the life cycle can be very helpful in understanding how the library functions day to day or hour by hour. This deeper level of understanding can provide managers a roadmap for devising improved services and streamlining processes. Workflows from one step of the life cycle to the next should flow seamlessly. They should be analyzed for ergonomics, redundancies, missing processes, and quality assurance.

Selection

If you ask selectors how they select items for inclusion in the collection, they may say that they read review journals and choose what to buy. In reality, there are a lot of steps taken between reading reviews and actually placing a title in an order cart. Let's detail those "missing" steps in a sample workflow analysis.

The best way to get a handle on this procedure is to start by interviewing the selectors. Create, in writing, the actual "how to" of the selection process. This can be a general outline. Once you have the overview, then begin to dig deeper. Fill in the details and ask about different steps. Don't expect to master the procedure immediately. Both the selector and the workflow analyst will remember different things at different times. As the details come together throughout the conversation, the workflow will be better understood. Avoid judging the process until the workflow has been detailed thoroughly.

The selection process is actually more complex than one might initially realize, even in a small library. Selectors have many avenues from which to choose materials. The analysis could begin with "Selectors consult *Publisher's Weekly*,

Booklist, and *Library Journal,* or even newspapers and popular magazines as review sources." That statement is then broken down even further: How often does the selector consult these resources? Where are the journals stored, and who has access? The analysis could continue with:

> These review journals come in the mail weekly or monthly, depending on the title. The member of staff who receives the title first staples a routing slip to the cover. The routing slip names all of the staff members who will share the title. When the first person finishes with it, he passes it to the next name on the list.

This tells us that in our example, library review journals are shared and that they are passed from one person to the next. We still need to know what selectors do with the journals while they are in their possession. Let's continue.

> As each selector reads a review journal, he writes his initials next to the titles he intends to add to the collection. Each selector is responsible for reading the portion of the journal that includes the subjects he selects for. Anyone can make suggestions to his fellow selectors for titles outside of his collection area by adding notes to the margin of any title in the journal. If that selector has already been crossed off the routing slip, the information can be shared directly through email, phone, or in person.

Now we know how selectors mark titles they intend to purchase for their own collection areas, as well as how they collaborate with selectors in other collection areas. The analysis is getting more and more refined the more we question exactly how each step is completed.

As selectors mark titles they intend to add to their own collections, they add the titles and publication information, such as ISBN and publication date, to a spreadsheet. This becomes the list that purchasers will order from. As titles are reviewed in various journals, the list also serves as a reminder of titles they already chose from a previous review.

One can see how analysis of each step of the selection process includes an action, such as making a list of titles to be purchased, and also a description of why that action is taken. As various selectors are interviewed about their process, different actions could be introduced (maybe one selector skips the list step and goes straight from reading reviews to placing titles in an online shopping cart with a vendor). As the actions and their explanations are analyzed, the efficiency of one process over another can be determined.

The last person on the routing slip places the review journals in a storage box kept at the reference desk. Anyone can refer back to these journals for up to a year, at which time the back issues are weeded.

This answers the question of where review journals are stored, who has access, and for how long.

Selectors organize their title selection lists by publication date. The month before a title is published, its publication information is submitted to the library's purchasers. This allows selectors to keep track of upcoming titles that they intend to purchase, but which may have been announced or reviewed too far in advance of its publication date to place an actual order at that time.

The process of selecting materials begins with finding out what titles are available and ends with making the final choice to purchase them. The goal of the selection workflow is to select materials for inclusion in the library collection, but there are budget and organization implications that will help selectors reach that goal efficiently. In our sample library, the process of keeping track of what has been selected and their costs falls within the selection workflow because the selectors are responsible for tracking that information.

> Selectors keep a budget spreadsheet for each collection for which they are responsible. When a title list is submitted to purchasers, selectors put the total cost of the order on their spreadsheet. As a double-check on pricing and availability, purchasers give each selector a print-out of their actual order summaries after they are submitted to the vendor.

Now we can see where two workflows overlap. Selectors have to keep an accurate budget tally so that they know the balance of their collection budget. However, if a different person submits a purchase to the vendor than who selected the titles, they must communicate details to each other and reconcile any changes or differences between the final order and the one submitted by the selector to the purchaser. They will also have to agree on who has authority to make last minute, executive decisions about the order. Can the purchaser make certain judgment calls on an order at the time it is placed, or do they need to consult with the selector every time any slight change comes up? For example, if the selector needs a title for a program by a certain date, but when the order is placed, the purchaser sees that it will not arrive on time from the chosen vendor. Can the purchaser find another vendor who will get the material to the selector on time – even if there is a small price difference between vendors? Or, should the purchaser ask permission, possibly holding up the order even longer while waiting for communication with the selector?

Another instance of overlap could be between two selectors. Selectors of different formats may want to communicate to each other which titles they plan to add to their collections. If a title is selected by the audio book selector, perhaps the selector for the e-book collection will choose different titles to diversify choices for library users. In a university, selectors for various disciplines might be interested to know that the same title is going to be used in two different classes for two different academic programs. To take this example full circle, when the titles arrive, catalogers may wonder why the same book has been assigned two completely different call numbers and question the selectors to find out if both of them intended to purchase the same title or if it was a mistake.

The "why" of selection – that is, why a particular title was chosen and another wasn't – is best addressed in the collection management policy. The selection workflow should address how often this policy is consulted. Does the policy exist only in form or do selectors consult it and review it as a regular part of the selection process? A library's collection management policy should outline some basics with regard to selection tools and selection goals. The goal of a collection policy is to set guidelines. Creating, using, and changing the policy will become part of the selection workflow. Ultimately, workflow is about fulfilling the objectives of policy and mission.

The above selection workflow analysis was arranged by activity, step by step. Another way to organize the analysis is by answering the questions "who, what, where, how, and when." Let's analyze a different workflow within selection in this way.

Something to consider in the selection process is how suggestions are made to the selector for adding materials to the collection. In many libraries, this can be as easy as someone asking the selector to purchase a particular item. The selector orders the item (through a variety of vendors or interlibrary loan) and makes sure that the person requesting the item gets access. (See Figure 2.1.)

Since the selector is the human point at which the decision is made, identify all the ways that suggestions are routed to this selector and the decision is made. You will notice that some questions fall into more than one category.

The selection process

| Demand |
| (Circulation and holds data, requests) |

| Library users | Faculty | Library staff |

| Collection management policy |

| Material reviews | Bestseller lists | Curriculum requirements |

| Selector |

| Choose vendor | Duplicate check | Consult budget |

| Material order |

Figure 2.1   Sample workflow for selection processes

Who

- Who creates/provides the suggestion form?
- Who can make a suggestion? Library users? Staff? Faculty? Non-residents?
- Who gets the suggestions once they are made?
- Can any staff member take a suggestion for any department?
- Who makes the purchase decision?
- Who lets the patron know that the item has been (or not been) acquired?

What

- What can be suggested: titles? Formats? Editions? Programming (speakers, classes, etc.)?

Where

- Where are suggestion slips or electronic forms housed: on the library's web site? In a box at the reference desk?
- Where are the requests stored until the decision is made?
- Where is the patron information stored so that they can be notified once the item is acquired?

How

- How are suggestions made? Is it a written form, or submitted by email or an electronic form? Verbally communicated? All of the above?
- How are patrons notified that the item is available?

When

- When (how often) are suggestions accepted?
- When are the materials purchased? Monthly? Quarterly?

Although this is presented in a "who, what, where, how, and when" format, try to keep the procedure as chronological as possible. Perhaps a "faculty member, student, or patron fills out a form requesting a book." Now the analysis begins. What happens next and with whom? Nail down the specifics. Name names and list dates, and if there is a question or a non-standard answer between employees in the same department, note this in your workflow. Non-standard answers or an unclear process should be investigated.

It is also important to visually observe the process to make sure all the steps are covered. Talking and consulting with the actual staff members performing the tasks is critical to understanding how the workflow functions. Often there is a disconnection between employees and employers in understanding who does what and when. Using observation and conversation with those directly involved will result in more accuracy than depending on someone else's impressions of the workflow. This can be a touchy subject with some people, construed as criticism rather than an unbiased detailing of the process. Analyzing workflows requires tact. The analyst should remain emotionally detached from the workflow. They make impartial observations, not judgments, so neutrality is important. New employees and outside consultants make great analysts because they have no emotional connections to the current procedures being followed by staff. The Kalamazoo (Michigan) Public Library hired someone with a background in lean process management in the manufacturing industry to analyze their workflows. They found that she did not bring pre-conceived notions about how libraries should or should not operate into the project of leaning their systems (Cornell, 2012).

In our example of the suggestions-for-purchase workflow, what is the goal? For staff members of a generic public library, this procedure's goal is to make sure that all suggestions are addressed and considered by the selector. The final decision to include the suggested item for the collection must still fit collection criteria. "The selector then follows up each suggestion with a personal letter, call, or email." This procedure appears on the face to reach the goal of addressing each suggestion. (Notice that the process goal was to *consider* all suggestions.)

Purchasing/acquisitions

Now that selections have been made, it is important to document the process of purchasing the selected items. How are vendors selected? What are the criteria for using a particular vendor? As with the selection process, detail the exact steps and who performs them. In general, some type of purchase order is created with a vendor, detailing the items to be purchased and at what cost. Additional charges, such as shipping and handling, would also be detailed. Depending on the library, this process can be multi-layered and include many departments. The workflow analyst will need to understand who orders the materials and how this is reconciled with the budgeting and payment systems in place.

An analysis of the purchasing workflow can be problematic. The purchasing and payment of library materials might involve outside, non-library departments with a very different agenda and mission than those of library employees. It is essential for anyone involved in the purchasing process to fully understand how bills are paid and items received. The larger the system, the more steps in place. This can sometimes cause problems between departments. It is important to tread carefully, especially when trying to determine processes beyond the scope of one's job or department. In all cases, regardless of the size or complexity of the organization, several things must happen.

1. An order is placed with a vendor

- Who places it?
- What procedure do they follow?
- Where is the paperwork or electronic file located, and who has access?
- Is approval required?

2. Items are shipped to the library (or to the library's designated receiver)

- Who actually receives the items?
- What happens to the shipping and receiving documents?
- Where do items go after they have been received by the library?
- How do they get processed and made ready for use?

3. Items are billed to the library and paid for by the library

- Who receives the bill?
- When is the bill paid?
- How and when is the library budget reconciled with the amount paid?

The above three items represent a skeleton of what must happen in any institution. To understand the purchasing workflow of a library, diagramming the people and departments responsible for the three areas listed above will be helpful. Larger institutions could have entire departments dedicated to each function, a workflow so complex that it is difficult to detail fully what happens with each item purchased. However, it is important to detail the procedure as closely as possible.

Understanding the purchasing workflow is essential for many practical reasons aside from obtaining materials. Clarifying procedures with the actual staff performing them can go a long way in understanding the entire process. The old adage of "walk a mile in my shoes" is particularly appropriate in dealing with the accounting and finance functions of an organization. Understanding the billing and payment process can facilitate relationships with the vendors and staff charged with managing the bookkeeping process. Timely payments and quick responses to problems can make the entire process smoother for library staff, and ultimately the library user.

The use of purchase orders can help libraries track their expenditures and tie them directly to specific items they purchase. A purchase order is a document used to itemize the terms of a purchase, such as how many items were bought and at what cost. It details who authorized the purchase and who the seller was. Purchase orders are numbered and dated, and specify what account the items are to be paid from. In a library setting, collections are often assigned a specific account name or number (as simple as "audio books" and "adult fiction" or more complicated with a number like "101" for fiction and then narrowed down to 101.1 for adult fiction, 101.2 for teen fiction, and 101.3 for youth fiction.). As mentioned above, sometimes the people that pay the bills are in an entirely different department than the people who receive the goods. The bill payers may never lay eyes on the actual purchased items. It is crucial in those instances that they know exactly what was purchased and what account to pay from. For library collection purchases, they probably do not need to know the actual titles of each item purchased by a library selector, but something like "30 audio books" or "25 fiction books" lets them know what they are paying for. Since each purchase order form is numbered, that number is used to track each phase of ordering and receiving the items. Paperwork is attached to the purchase order at each step: an order summary, a packing slip that details the items received, and a copy of the invoice that was paid. This verifies that what is paid for matches what was ordered and received. Library staff need to be careful, especially when spending tax-payer's money, to carefully and clearly document what they spent the money on. Accountability is important to a transparent and trustworthy organization.

Purchase orders also help staff troubleshoot the purchasing system. When items are received, it helps staff figure out who gets them and where they go next. If an unexpected box of items is delivered, the library will be able to track its purpose by looking at the purchase order number on the packing slip. Occasionally, invoices arrive before the goods do. Tracking the purchase order number will verify if the items were received yet. Accounting software or the library's ILS can be used to automate this tracking process, or a simple paper log book that documents each purchase order used. The purchase order workflow should indicate how purchase orders are tracked, from the time the order is placed to the check written for payment (and even beyond, to the check clearing the bank account). (See Figure 2.2.)

Accounting and finance functions have reporting and processing requirements that may be helpful to library staff

Figure 2.2   Sample purchase order

trying to amass data on collections. Understanding the goals of a financial report and the information needs of those charged with reporting accounting functions can be very helpful to those who manage library collections. Both departments use purchasing data, so there may be redundancy in data collection. For example, financial reporters need to know how many items were purchased and at what cost. Selectors need to keep track of how much of their budget was spent, and in what subjects or formats. Both departments are working from the same set of data. Cooperation between them can give more meaning to the numbers and more efficiency in data gathering when they share information.

Specifically, let's take a fictional public library suffering from declining revenue, but increasing need. Financial managers have articulated a need to cut collection budgets significantly. At the same time, selectors have determined that there is an increasing need (from requests or circulation data) for career and job search materials. That analysis has also indicated a declining need for leisure-oriented items such as travel and investment titles. Combining the library's financial and collection data allows both departments to be responsive to the changing needs of the community and the library. Money can be moved around from one line of the budget to another, and staff can see where there was leftover money in past fiscal years. The knowledge and understanding of data gathered during the purchasing workflow directly leads to an ability to manage both collections and costs in a declining budget.

Processing

Once the materials have arrived, they enter the processing part of the life cycle. Processing refers to the technical services department or person in a library that prepares an item for cataloging, circulation, and shelving in the library collection. Different libraries have different names for that procedure, but essentially this is the person or department that unpacks the materials and readies them for library use. The type and size of the library could determine how this is accomplished. In general someone must:

1. Unpack the materials.
2. Decide which collection will house them (reference, large print, audio, maps, etc.).
3. Direct how the processing of that item will be handled.
4. Create a catalog record or link it to an existing one.

Each of the above has its own workflow. Special libraries and university collections can have extremely detailed procedures for each. Cataloging complex items can be difficult, and adherence to standards can be problematic for catalogers and staff. For any library, this is the last stop before items are released to the users. Good cataloging and proper processing can make the difference between an item that is used and retrievable in the catalog and one that is not.

For each collection, there should be a standard required for processing. Although collections should be defined in terms of shelving area for labeling, physical format dictates the processing standard. With the advance of multiple formats available, it is short sighted to imagine only a few types of items being processed in libraries. Consider a public library non-fiction collection. Perhaps the library interfiles books, audio books, and documentary DVDs in the same shelf space. The cataloging of each item indicates its location in the non-fiction collection, but the physical format determines things like cases, wrappings, and sticker placement.

Processing has a couple of components worth mentioning at this time. Many libraries use stickers as finding aids and also as shelving identifiers. All staff members need to be aware of what each sticker means. A public library sticker could help patrons differentiate science fiction novels from mystery novels and help shelvers determine in which collection an item belongs. Consistency in utilizing these methods is important. Use of finding aids versus shelving aids can cause confusion among both staff and patrons. If there is a mystery sticker used in the youth collection, and that same sticker is used to define an adult audio book as a mystery title, make sure all people are aware of the differences. Perhaps genres are interfiled in the audio book collection, but separated in the book collection. When someone sees

"Audio Book Mystery" in the catalog, they need to know on which shelf to look for the item. Is it interfiled with mystery books? Is there a separate mystery section in audio books?

The goal of processing is to make items shelf-ready. Analysis of the processing workflow can be extremely detailed and often frustrating. The more formats and collections a library has, the more issues with managing the workflow. At this point, it is probably helpful to formulate subdivisions in the collection. In the workflow, each item type, as well as collection, must be considered separately. For example, let's say that a youth department in a public library purchases a DVD for a parenting collection. Are these DVDs treated differently than other DVDs in the youth collection? Are they treated differently from DVDs shelved in the adult collection? When diagramming the workflow for processing, consider the types of items and the collections where the items ultimately reside.

Cataloging and linking have workflows separate from processing, but are another example of where workflows overlap. Catalogers create or find a record for the library's ILS that helps searchers find items owned by the library. A cataloging workflow begins with the item: what is it (which format) and which one (the exact title). It continues with how the cataloger creates a new record if original cataloging is to be performed. That would include details of where they get the items they catalog (perhaps they catalog items that appear on a certain shelf in their work area, put there by processors at the end of their workflow), where they perform the cataloging (at their own desk or at a specific, designated workstation), and which software they use. The workflow would continue with how the software works, which features of the software they use and don't use (and why), down to the actual cataloging rules they follow. If copy cataloging is performed, there may be a different set of procedures followed. Once a catalog record is created or found, the workflow turns to linking the item to the record.

Linking is often the last step before items are made available to the public. Someone has to create a holding to the catalog record and enter the specifics of where the item can be found in the library. Perhaps linking is done by the same people that do cataloging, or perhaps it is an entirely different department. The linking workflow includes things like:

- Who performs linking?
- What software do they use? Is it a module of the library's automation system? Does it require a separate log-in from other parts of the system?
- When are items linked? Are they linked before or after they are processed?
- Where does linking take place? Where are items found that need linking? Where are items placed once the link is created?
- How long does it take to link an item to a record?

Each institution will have its own workflow depending on its physical space, the types of items they typically catalog and link, and the makeup of the staff that perform these tasks.

Shelving

Shelving is often an unsung and unnoticed process in a library. Good shelving practices and good shelvers are essential to a quality library collection. Although this is done by a group of often the lowest paid staff in a library setting, it can make or break a library in terms of how efficiently items are found and used by the public and staff. Good shelving involves utilizing effective training and consistent processing of materials so that shelvers can tell at a glance where something belongs in the library. The shelving process itself, from sorting, carting, and moving items around the library, should be looked at closely by library staff. As one of the most physical jobs in the library setting, ergonomic aspects of shelving should be closely examined and analyzed. Even simple tasks such as sorting and checking the physical condition of materials before carting, can save steps and move items more efficiently through the library.

Shelving is a unique point in the circulation of materials because an actual human is touching each item and keeping the physical order of the collection. This function is critical to the entire life cycle of the library. Shelvers and processors are usually the first line of attack in promoting the physical quality of a collection. Processing and technical services are about making an item shelf ready. Shelvers use the information placed on the materials by processors to put items in the correct place. Shelving failure can push a library into chaos. Even if other parts of collection quality are ignored, this part is essential in even the most understaffed libraries. Assessment of materials and auditing should be an integral part of the training of processors and shelvers.

The goal of library processing and its companion workflow, shelving, is to assist people in identifying and properly storing items. Deviation from this workflow can be problematic. In the use of finding aids, a misplaced or misused sticker can cause a patron to not get exactly what they are looking for. It can also cause an item to be processed as one thing and shelved or cataloged as another. Ultimately, item processing can be a key factor in missing or misshelved items.

Analysis of the shelving process begins when an item is newly added to the collection or when a previously checked out item is returned and ready to begin the circulation system again. In some libraries, shelving activities also include re-shelving items that have been used but not checked out. To thoroughly analyze the shelving workflow, begin with how the shelvers find the material to re-shelve: at the moment that an item is returned to the library, or when a new item is ready for shelving.

- How did the item get to the shelving station or area?
- Who brought it?
- Are items sorted while in the shelving station, or somewhere else?
- What is the turnaround time from return of the item to its placement on the shelf?

Because this is usually more labor intensive and requires physical movement of the materials, it will be helpful in creating a workflow that pays special attention to the "how" of this process. Smaller libraries can have dramatically different procedures from larger libraries based on physical storage and size. High circulating libraries, regardless of physical size, can also have dramatically different issues with shelving and turnover. Issues of quality control, training, processing standards, and ergonomics often converge at the shelving point of the life cycle.

Shelving is an area where lean process management principles can benefit hugely. The founders of the Lean Enterprise Institute describe lean: "The core idea is to maximize customer value while minimizing waste. Simply, lean means creating more value for customers with fewer resources." (Lean Enterprise Institute, 2013). Returned items that linger for days or weeks before they are shelved are an example of waste: a waste of time and a waste of the items themselves. Improving turnaround time on re-shelving items improves value for customers, and if this process can be achieved with the fewest resources – staff, carts, shelves, elevators, steps, handling of materials, etc. – then it is truly a lean process.

Circulation

After materials are processed and shelved, they await the arrival of someone to use them. Items are checked out, or used in-house, by patrons and then re-shelved. In some instances this can happen several times in a day, a week, or hardly at all. Each collection has its own rhythm and use that is appropriate for its type. A popular, new release DVD might have hundreds of check outs (circulations) in a few months, whereas a dictionary or very specific reference book might only be used once in a while.

Such item use and reuse is an essential component of using a library. This is where the library's users most closely interact with the collection. Circulation activities are usually labor intensive and are points in the life cycle where customer service is paramount. Close attention to this continuous cycle of use and re-use is important to both staff and the users, and should be a major consideration in any library management plan.

Library use is defined by circulation. In a public library, for example, this can be a new, best-selling fiction book. A library user checks out the library book. The item is charged to the card holder's account. After a specified time, the book is returned and the process is repeated with a different person. This routine is repeated until an item is weeded (retired and removed from the collection). The circulation workflow should be analyzed from checkout to return and all the possible deviations that can occur during that process.

Although most staffers and even the general public are aware of this basic procedure of circulation, the analysis is still important and should be detailed. The inclusion of library automation software (its ILS) that tracks circulation is an essential part of the analysis. Even the most basic checkout and return should be detailed.

Items to be considered:

- How long is the lending period?

- What does the ILS, or library policy, consider a circulation or use?

- Are all items treated the same by the ILS?

- Are all borrowers subject to the same rules?

- What tracking statistics are generated by the ILS and what do they mean?

In order to get a handle on the circulation workflow, begin with a simple scenario and document each step. What happens when someone checks out a book? The patron presents a valid library card and the computer system registers that patron's account. The book's barcode is entered into the system and a checkout period is assigned. The patron departs with the item. If there are security measures, such as RFID or tattle tape that requires staff to demagnetize or shut off security on an item, that process should also be detailed.

In addition, any deviation from the expected use behavior should be addressed. For example, what happens if an item is damaged upon return? What happens when a patron wants to extend their check-out time? How are reserves handled? It is also important to examine areas that might be outside the traditional routine, such as an interlibrary loan request or the use of archival or special collections.

Circulation is related to how the library keeps track of its holdings. Where the materials are, and how they got there, is essential knowledge for collection quality. Think about some of the daily tasks everyone takes for granted in a library. If a patron or staff member looks up an item in the online catalog, the expectation is that the item is where the system says it is. Is it checked out? Is it lost or missing? Is it shelved in the place where the catalog says it should be? If these activities are not accurately reflected in the online catalog, or if staff have no confidence in the system, then the library has failed in its organizational objective. Librarians, in turn, have failed in their objective to be custodians of the materials.

It is also important to approach this workflow analysis from both a patron account point of view and from the item's current location or status. Can items be tracked through the system regardless of their status? Is patron activity detailed on the patron's account, and can it be tracked via the card holder? What happens when someone returns a checked out item? In general, this is probably a reverse of the above process; however, you cannot assume that and must still detail the entire return process. Careful consideration should be paid to the actual flow of the items.

As this analysis takes shape you will have greater insight into the workings of libraries, and patterns and expectations will emerge. Data patterns with respect to how items move through the library system can provide a great deal of insight into how the library functions. As these workflows are detailed, it will be possible to improve efficiency and highlight trouble areas. In addition, the lack of such data is a flag for further investigation: is an item missing? Cataloged improperly? Shelved improperly? Is the title appropriate for current collection needs? Has anyone physically looked at the item? An item's very existence can be called into question. The circulation workflow is a map to quality collection management: every item in its place, used, and serving the library's stated collection goal.

Periodically installing quick quality checks throughout the workflow can give the librarian additional data in usage and the movement of materials through the library. There are also some side benefits to this analysis of your data. Library management, regardless of size, should continually monitor processes to make sure the appropriate people are doing the appropriate job. Implementing periodic checks on your system can facilitate an overall improvement of efficiency, which ultimately translates into collection quality.

Weeding

Weeding is one of those subjects that everyone agrees on, in theory. In practice, however, this can be the subject of hot debate. It is helpful to think of weeding as the opposite of selection. Adding items to the collection that are appropriate and which serve the mission and collection policy of the library is pretty straightforward. The trouble comes when either the mission of a library changes, patronage changes, or the item is no longer viable for the intended purpose. This can sound overwhelming, but if you think of items, even at the point of purchase or selection, as having a limited shelf life, it becomes easier to understand the subtleties of weeding.

Lack of weeding has the potential to drag down an entire collection's performance by having outdated materials crowd out newer, more relevant items. Shelf space is a fixed amount for many libraries, so weeding becomes a matter of making room so that newer items have space. Just as in selection, a concerted effort must be made to discuss standards for weeding. Standards can vary from collection to collection and from library to library. Circulation and holding data, as well as curriculum needs, are important tools in the creation of de-selection standards.

Weeding is often done on an as-needed basis by many libraries. Changes in communities or selection standards often change so slowly or in such subtle ways that this important aspect of collection maintenance gets forgotten or de-emphasized. It is also difficult to communicate to the general public what weeding is to avoid public relations nightmares. Books and other library items are often seen as a permanent record of history instead of a useful item with a limited shelf life. Libraries can find themselves stuck between trying to keep everything and continuing to add to the collection.

Staff members have to take leadership in talking about the goals of a collection. Every library, from a small public library with popular materials to a large research institution, will have goals and objectives for the collection they manage. Weeding often implies throwing something away. Often, it means that this item is no longer useful where it is and it needs to move somewhere else. For a small public library with several copies of a best seller from a few years ago, it might mean weeding four copies for a book sale and keeping one for future use. For a university it might mean moving something from a circulating collection to a storage area for future research needs. Educating both staff and library users on the finer points of information currency and accuracy should be a part of training. When library staff can explain their collection goals to the public, it can make a huge difference in avoiding misunderstandings about collection maintenance.

Although this workflow falls by the wayside in many libraries, items must be removed from the collection for various reasons. The "how" part of this process needs to be documented in detail. The "why" and "when" of weeding might be best addressed in the collection management policy. However, on-going de-selection should be documented in a workflow analysis. For example, if a librarian runs a report monthly on old or low-circulating items to find possible candidates for weeding, that process should be detailed. After running the report, perhaps the librarian pulls specific items off of the shelf. They might pass the items to another person in another department to delete the holding in the library catalog, or they might do that themselves. Procedures as mundane as crossing out barcodes and removing security stickers need to be included in the workflow. Is a particular color marker used to cross out the barcodes? Can security stickers or other parts (such as cases) be re-used? Are the weeded items then passed on to the folks who sell them in a book sale, or are they recycled? Where are they stored between book sales? Remember, the goal of this workflow is to remove items from the collection that are no longer useful. If the workflow turns out to have extra steps that have nothing to do with this goal, the procedure should be revised. If staff are unclear on the answers to any of these questions, it is also a flag for workflow revision.

Workflow analysis improves efficiency

Now that all the work is documented, it is time to look more broadly at library operations. Organize each workflow into a sequence. Sometimes a floor plan is helpful when looking at a process. Where are your items and how do they get where they need to be? Drawing a line following the material flow in your building gives perspective to the physical layout and staff organization. Minimizing the number of times items are moved saves labor and is more ergonomic for workers. Taking a step back and looking at the overall flow of materials through the library will indicate any inefficiency.

Within each workflow, examine the core activity of each step. What is the goal? What is the process? Are there checks on quality? Are there redundancies in the process? Could steps be combined to improve efficiency? Not all of these

Understanding your workflow

questions will have obvious answers, but examining the details will provide management and staff with a much better view of how the library is operating. Details add up to a whole. The pieces need to add up to a logical workflow, and the workflows together should result in a quality collection.

There is also a flip side to this view of the process. Imagine if duties were separated and changed. Could quality be improved if staff acted as a check on each other's work? The application of physical inventory is an example of an extra quality control step. Physical inventory, which will be explored in greater detail in a later chapter, can be a quality check on the processing and cataloging workflows. Adding an inventory check, performed by a different person than the original processor and cataloger, can upgrade the quality of the materials hitting the shelves. If the inventory date can be recorded in the item record through the ILS, items will be marked as having passed an "inspection" of sorts. Staff will know that on the date the item was inventoried, it passed muster.

There should also be consideration given to how people function in these jobs. For many employees, repetitive work can be problematic and cause a decline in performance. For others, repetitive work can be more productive. Consideration of the skills and attitudes of those charged with certain responsibilities within a workflow can pay off in quality improvement. Setting standards of performance can also be helpful to a supervisor. These standards can become measurable benchmarks in performance and allow for immediate feedback to employees.

The critical questions

Every staff member can participate in the quality control process in a library. Every time a member of staff comes in contact with a library item, they should be able to answer critical questions about it. Even in small libraries, the sheer volume of materials moving through the system will require all staff to be empowered to address deviations from the standards. Failure to recognize them or act on them will prevent quality control. Anything from a torn cover to a poorly cataloged item should be flagged and dealt with procedurally. Standards should be evaluated from time to time in order to regularly address changes in staff and procedures. These are the critical questions:

- Was the physical preparation of the book performed to the standard?
- Was the linking of the item to its bibliographic record performed correctly?
- Does the item listed in the catalog reflect the item in hand?
- Is the status of the item accurately reflected in the catalog?

The critical questions are not designed to identify a fault or a perpetrator. It should be assumed that no one can process, catalog, or shelve perfectly every single time. Even a small library has thousands of items to manage. Mistakes are bound to occur. These critical questions look at trends and identify the effectiveness of procedures. The point is to detail what is actually happening and compare it to what should be happening. They also identify communication gaffes and training gaps. Again, many components of employee/employer relationships, work process design, and communication might be at issue. A workflow might be just fine, but adherence, training, or quality control checks might not be implemented properly.

Quality begins with a thorough understanding of the workflows in the library. Detailing each process and analyzing them is instrumental in developing appropriate training and standards. All levels of staff need to participate in the workflow analysis and understand the motive of working toward a quality collection. It is important to recognize that as the library's mission or service population changes, and even formats of media change, the library's workflows will also adapt. Preparing for this requires vigilance and a healthy plan for collection auditing and quality maintenance.

Collection metrics

Abstract: Collection metrics is about measuring a library collection. Common metrics in libraries include circulation, collection age, and collection use. This chapter looks at accuracy and error rates of catalog records in integrated library systems, and using a statistical sample to audit the collection.

Key words: metrics, measurement, data, circulation, collection activity, integrated library, system, accuracy, confidence interval, collection age, collection use.

Now that we have an understanding of how materials flow through a library, we can discuss measuring that flow. A metric is a system or standard of measurement. In a later chapter we will talk about statistics, which are facts surmised by analyzing metrics. In other words, first we need to gather the data (metrics), and then we will use that data to evaluate our libraries and collections through statistics.

The circulation metric

The most common library metric is circulation. In order to truly make conclusions about the collection, one must understand how and what is being counted when a circulation is tallied and reported by the ILS. This is actually fairly complicated because a circulation is not simply a check-out, but may also include renewals, in-house use, and check-in. Let's illustrate this with a typical library transaction.

Item A is checked out to a patron. The ILS tallies a single check-out. Three weeks later, the item is returned to the library. The ILS tallies a check-in. Here we have two distinct activities: the item being checked out and the item being checked in. In this simple transaction, what constitutes a "circulation?" Is it the circle of check-out and check-in taken together as one measurement? Or does this transaction result in two separate measurements – a check-out and a check-in? What if there is a renewal between check-out and check-in? Is that a third measurement, or is it still part of the single "circulation?" It is important to clarify the definition of words like "circulation" to ensure accurate data.

For example, it could be important to distinguish between check-outs at the staff counter vs. check-outs on the self-checkout machine. In large libraries with multiple service points, measuring check-outs at certain desks or on certain floors reveals information about building use. Renewals, placing items on hold, and in-library use also detail collection activity, but these particular metrics are often used interchangeably with the term "circulation."

There are also implications for libraries that migrate to a new ILS. Will the new system count library transactions in the same way the old system did? Will previous data match up with new data in order to continue to make decisions about the library and its collections?

It is important to recognize that different departments will require different kinds of metrics. For the purposes of reporting to the general public or a board of directors, a circulation metric might total these check-in/check-out/renewal library transactions together, with the goal of measuring overall library activity. Collection managers, on the other hand, will want more detailed information about how their collections are used. An item with 50 registered "circulations" could break down to something like 30 check-outs, 20 renewals, and 50 check-ins. On the other hand, it could mean only 50 check-outs and not count renewals at all. A collection manager should be aware that items that are renewed almost as many times as they are checked out are an indication that few people can manage to finish using these titles in one check-out cycle. These items may be given longer due-dates, more copies may be purchased, or they may be re-assigned to a different collection with different circulation rules if the collection manager is aware of the renewal metric within circulation. Similarly, items that perpetually have check-outs on their records, but not check-ins should also be flagged. Perhaps a library will require a money deposit in order to check those items out in the future, or perhaps they will be labeled for in-house use only.

The bottom line is that circulation means use of the collection. The ILS circulation report should include:

■ Number of check-outs.

■ Number of renewals.

■ Number of in-house uses.

■ Number of times the item was lent in interlibrary loan (ILL).

Electronic collections must also be counted as used. This includes metrics like database remote log-ins and e-book downloads. Databases and e-books are part of the library's collection, and must be counted as used. Libraries may or may not want to separate these metrics from other collection use. For example, the ability to compare the use of a title in e-book format to the use of its print counterpart may indicate patron preference and have budgeting implications. If the e-book platform only counts downloads and not "returns," the collection manager needs to understand that 50 circulations (25 check-ins and 25 check-outs? 50 check-outs? 40 check-outs and 10 renewals?) of the print copy may not be the same thing as 50 downloads of the electronic copy.

There is also danger in using the circulation metric for an overall indication of library activity. This is not appropriate when we consider library use that is not tracked by the ILS. Meeting room use, library program attendance, and computer and equipment use, used in conjunction with circulation data, will provide a more accurate measure of library activity than a single metric like circulation.

Other collection metrics

There are two kinds of metrics. The first are those that describe the activity of items as a group. They are used to answer questions like:

- How are youth nonfiction science titles performing compared to the overall performance of youth nonfiction?
- How old is the youth science collection (on average)?
- How does the use of downloadable materials compare to print?
- What items are more likely to be stolen or damaged?

Other metrics describe individual items. They are used to answer questions like:

- How does the use of Title A compare to the use of similar titles?
- How old is Title A?
- What is the physical condition of Title A?

- Is there updated information in a different title, or a newer edition of Title A?

Metrics answer these questions with unbiased data about the collection. Metrics should serve as a major factor in making selections, weeding, and other decisions about the collection. Standards can be instituted on a library-wide basis and calculated consistently regardless of changes in management, ILS system, or staff.

Collection audit

No collection can be adequately analyzed without good data. For collection managers, most often our data set for these metrics comes from the library catalog (the ILS). All collection items in the library are described in the catalog. It is the main search tool for both staff and patrons. The accuracy of the catalog is of paramount concern to any library. In the chapter about workflow analysis, we suggested that some of these problems can be both detected and solved through a close look at internal workflows. Having solved those workflow issues, now it is time to look closer at the collection itself and clean up past mistakes. Just as workflows were audited, so must the collection be.

Anecdotal evidence is the first sign that a collection has quality concerns. Patrons or staff may complain that they cannot locate an item, or that they have to continually order certain items on interlibrary loan for patrons. Additional signs could be a long list of missing or lost items, or an excessive number of patrons claiming they have returned items that are still on their account. Even the inadvertent purchasing of unwanted duplicate titles could indicate collection quality problems.

Statistical sample

While this chapter focuses on metrics and a later chapter deals with statistics, we must now set the stage for deciding if further intervention such as a physical inventory is necessary. We have decided that there is enough anecdotal information to indicate that we should proceed further, and this is the next step.

The use of simple statistics is helpful in making general conclusions about the entire group, or *population*. Libraries use catalog holdings as the population for statistical purposes. For a large research or university library, holdings can number in the millions. Even a smaller library probably has holdings numbering in the thousands. Essentially, what statistics do is to allow us to make conclusions about the whole population by looking at relatively few randomly selected items.

Let's use the example of a medium sized public library with a variety of media formats in its collection. One of the staff members feels that there are problems with the catalog's information. She feels that there are mismarked items, as well as items that are indicated by the catalog to be one format or title but are actually another. This member of staff would like to do a cursory examination to see if there is an error rate that indicates an actual problem. The strategy is to sample the catalog and then see how many errors are present. With this information, she will report to her manager and develop a plan to address the issues found.

The total number of all items in the collection as indicated by the library catalog is 71,000. This number includes everything from periodicals to e-books. Anything with a barcode or which has been cataloged is included as part of the population. This example library has a total population of 71,000. The goal is to establish, from a small piece of the collection, that most of the 71,000 items are correctly represented in the catalog and that they are shelved where indicated.

The reality is that no one actually physically counted all the items, so we can't know if this number is correct. We do have 71,000 records which should, in theory, match the physical holdings. Reality would dictate that this number is probably incorrect for many reasons: lost or stolen items, damaged items, duplicate records, or items that were removed physically but their catalog records never purged. All of these instances will change the total number of records and physical items that actually exist.

How many items and records should someone examine to get a sense of how the library catalog is performing? This is where statistics gives us the edge. Obviously, the more records and holdings examined, the more confident we can be about making generalizations. It is important to calculate a *sample size* (the number of items to actually be examined) that will give enough information to make our conclusions reasonable. Familiarity with a few terms will help.

Population: Again, this is the total number of items in our defined group from which our sample will be drawn. In examining the catalog, this would be all of the records in the catalog or possibly all the records in a single collection. For instance, if you want to make a claim about how many DVDs are scratched, you only need to sample from DVDs, not the entire collection.

Confidence interval: This number is expressed as a plus or minus figure, usually given as an error rate range. For example, when quoting polls, "40 percent of the people polled will vote for candidate X, plus or minus 4 percent." The 4 percent refers to the confidence interval, or how much error might be in the statement. In essence,

Candidate X will get a percentage of votes ranging from 36 percent (40 – 4) to 44 percent (40 + 4).

Confidence level: Expressed as a level of how certain you are of the answer: "I am 95 percent certain that this answer is accurate." Most researchers use the 95 percent confidence level. It's also a baseline requirement for a claim. For example, you won't conclude that your mysteries aren't circulating unless your resulting statistics agree to this confidence level.

Sample: A subset of the population that is manageable in size on which one can perform measurements. It is hopefully large enough to make meaningful statistical conclusions.

Sample size: The number of items in a sample.

In our library collection example, sample size will refer to the number of records examined to generalize about the entire catalog. Intuitively, it can be understood that the more records examined, the better the accuracy. However, to be effective, the sample must be truly random. In other words, you can't move up and down the aisles pulling books off of the shelves and expect a truly random sample. Remember, a portion of the population is in circulation. Truly random samples must be generated from all the items in the population, regardless of their current circulation status.

The math behind generating a sample size is fairly complicated. Web sites such as *ehow.com* and the U.S. Department of Health and Human Services (*hrsa.gov*) do a good job of explaining the formula. However, generating a random sample is easy with the help of free online sample size generators, such as Survey System (Creative Research Systems, available at *surveysystem.com*). Simply enter your confidence level, confidence interval, and population and the tool will calculate your sample size for you. According to Survey System, the number of randomly selected records based on a population of 71,000 using a confidence interval of 4 percent and a confidence level of 95 percent is 595. Another free sample size calculator is available at the National Statistical Service website (*nss.gov.au*). Their calculator is a bit more detailed, but just as effective. (See Figure 3.1.)

There are also free online tools that can help with the next step, which is choosing which 595 records to include in the sample. One example of a random sample generator is Research Randomizer (Urbaniak and Plous, *randomizer. org*). This tool will help you choose which 595 records to look at. Tell the randomizer to generate one set of numbers with 595 unique numbers in the set. The range will be from 1 to 71,000. Set the generator to sort the resulting random numbers in order from least to greatest. The generator creates a list of 595 random numbers between 1 and 71,000.

Sample Size Calculator

This Sample Size Calculator is presented as a public service of Creative Research Systems survey software. You can use it to determine how many people you need to interview in order to get results that reflect the target population as precisely as needed. You can also find the level of precision you have in an existing sample.

Before using the sample size calculator, there are two terms that you need to know. These are: **confidence interval** and **confidence level**. If you are not familiar with these terms, click here. To learn more about the factors that affect the size of confidence intervals, click here.

Enter your choices in a calculator below to find the sample size you need or the confidence interval you have. Leave the Population box blank, if the population is very large or unknown.

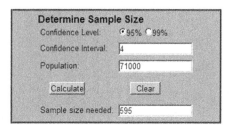

Determine Sample Size	
Confidence Level:	⦿ 95% ◯ 99%
Confidence Interval:	4
Population:	71000
Calculate	Clear
Sample size needed:	595

Figure 3.1 Screen shot from *surveysystem.com* determining sample size

It may be a bit tedious, but take a numbered collection shelf list (depending on how your ILS outputs a shelf list, you may want to export it to spreadsheet software) and mark the records for each number generated. For example, if the randomizer chose numbers 882, 24644, and 68314, use those records on the shelf list as part of the sample (see Figures 3.2 and 3.3).

Carefully compare the sample items to their current shelf status, call number, format, and other catalog information. Errors may include data entry mistakes such as wrong call numbers, misspellings, incorrect format, and wrong circulation rules (such as item marked as non-circulating reference when it should be a regular circulating item). This

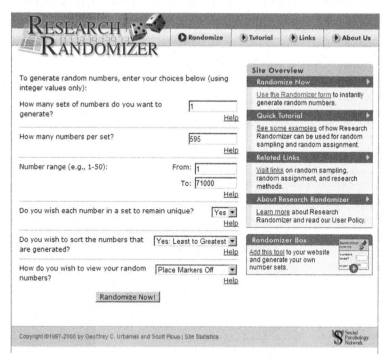

Figure 3.2 Screen shot of Research Randomizer's random number generator form

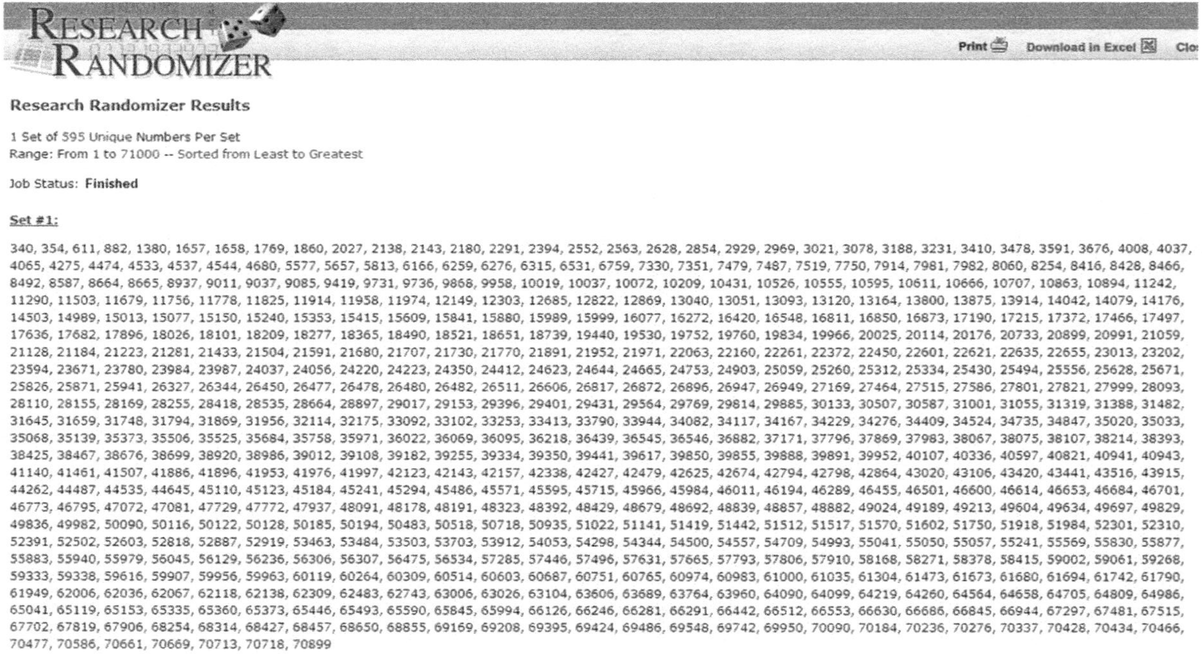

RESEARCH RANDOMIZER

Research Randomizer Results

1 Set of 595 Unique Numbers Per Set
Range: From 1 to 71000 -- Sorted from Least to Greatest

Job Status: **Finished**

Set #1:

340, 354, 611, 882, 1380, 1657, 1658, 1769, 1860, 2027, 2138, 2143, 2180, 2291, 2394, 2552, 2563, 2628, 2854, 2929, 2969, 3021, 3078, 3188, 3231, 3410, 3478, 3591, 3676, 4008, 4037, 4065, 4275, 4474, 4533, 4537, 4544, 4680, 5377, 5657, 5813, 6166, 6259, 6276, 6315, 6531, 6759, 7330, 7351, 7479, 7487, 7519, 7750, 7914, 7981, 7982, 8060, 8254, 8416, 8428, 8466, 8492, 8587, 8664, 8665, 8937, 9011, 9037, 9085, 9419, 9731, 9736, 9858, 9958, 10019, 10037, 10072, 10209, 10431, 10526, 10555, 10595, 10611, 10666, 10707, 10863, 10894, 11242, 11290, 11503, 11679, 11756, 11778, 11825, 11914, 11958, 11974, 12149, 12303, 12685, 12822, 12869, 13040, 13051, 13093, 13120, 13164, 13800, 13875, 13914, 14042, 14079, 14176, 14503, 14989, 15013, 15077, 15150, 15240, 15353, 15415, 15609, 15841, 15880, 15989, 16077, 16272, 16420, 16548, 16811, 16850, 16873, 17190, 17215, 17372, 17466, 17497, 17636, 17682, 17896, 18026, 18101, 18209, 18277, 18365, 18490, 18521, 18651, 18739, 19440, 19530, 19752, 19760, 19834, 19966, 20025, 20114, 20176, 20733, 20899, 20991, 21059, 21128, 21184, 21223, 21281, 21433, 21504, 21591, 21680, 21707, 21730, 21770, 21891, 21952, 21971, 22063, 22160, 22261, 22372, 22450, 22601, 22621, 22635, 23013, 23202, 23594, 23671, 23780, 23984, 23987, 24037, 24056, 24220, 24223, 24350, 24412, 24623, 24644, 24665, 24753, 24903, 25059, 25260, 25312, 25334, 25430, 25494, 25556, 25628, 25671, 25826, 25871, 25941, 26327, 26344, 26450, 26477, 26478, 26480, 26482, 26511, 26606, 26817, 26872, 26896, 26947, 26949, 27169, 27464, 27515, 27586, 27801, 27821, 27999, 28093, 28110, 28155, 28169, 28255, 28418, 28535, 28664, 28897, 29017, 29153, 29396, 29401, 29431, 29954, 29769, 29814, 29885, 30133, 30507, 30587, 31001, 31055, 31319, 31388, 31482, 31645, 31659, 31748, 31794, 31869, 31956, 32114, 32175, 33092, 33102, 33253, 33413, 33790, 33944, 34082, 34117, 34167, 34229, 34276, 34409, 34524, 34735, 34847, 35020, 35033, 35068, 35139, 35373, 35506, 35525, 35684, 35758, 35971, 36022, 36069, 36095, 36218, 36439, 36545, 36546, 36882, 37171, 37796, 37869, 37983, 38067, 38075, 38107, 38214, 38393, 38425, 38467, 38676, 38699, 38920, 38986, 39012, 39108, 39182, 39255, 39334, 39350, 39441, 39617, 39850, 39855, 39888, 39891, 39952, 40107, 40336, 40597, 40821, 40941, 40943, 41140, 41461, 41507, 41886, 41896, 41953, 41976, 41997, 42123, 42143, 42157, 42338, 42427, 42479, 42625, 42674, 42794, 42798, 42864, 43020, 43106, 43420, 43441, 43516, 43915, 44262, 44441, 44535, 44645, 45110, 45123, 45184, 45241, 45594, 45486, 45571, 45595, 45715, 45946, 45984, 46011, 46194, 46289, 46455, 46501, 46600, 46614, 46653, 46684, 46701, 46773, 46795, 47072, 47081, 47229, 47772, 47937, 48091, 48118, 48191, 48323, 48392, 48429, 48679, 48692, 48839, 48857, 48882, 49024, 49189, 49213, 49604, 49634, 49697, 49829, 49836, 49982, 50090, 50116, 50122, 50128, 50185, 50194, 50483, 50518, 50718, 50935, 51022, 51141, 51419, 51442, 51512, 51517, 51570, 51602, 51730, 51918, 51984, 52301, 52310, 52391, 52502, 52603, 52818, 52887, 52919, 53463, 53484, 53503, 53703, 53912, 54053, 54298, 54344, 54500, 54557, 54709, 54993, 55041, 55050, 55057, 55241, 55569, 55830, 55877, 55883, 55940, 55979, 56045, 56129, 56236, 56306, 56307, 56475, 56534, 57285, 57446, 57496, 57631, 57665, 57793, 57806, 57910, 58168, 58271, 58378, 58415, 59002, 59061, 59268, 59333, 59338, 59616, 59907, 59956, 59963, 60119, 60264, 60309, 60514, 60603, 60687, 60751, 60765, 60974, 60983, 61000, 61035, 61304, 61473, 61673, 61680, 61694, 61742, 61790, 61949, 62006, 62036, 62067, 62118, 62138, 62309, 62483, 62743, 63006, 63026, 63104, 63606, 63689, 63764, 63960, 64090, 64099, 64219, 64260, 64564, 64658, 64705, 64809, 64986, 65041, 65119, 65153, 65335, 65360, 65373, 65446, 65493, 65590, 65845, 65994, 66126, 66246, 66281, 66291, 66442, 66512, 66553, 66630, 66686, 66845, 66944, 67297, 67481, 67515, 67702, 67819, 67906, 68254, 68314, 68427, 68457, 68650, 68855, 69169, 69208, 69395, 69424, 69486, 69548, 69742, 69950, 70090, 70184, 70236, 70276, 70337, 70428, 70434, 70466, 70477, 70586, 70661, 70669, 70713, 70718, 70899

Figure 3.3 Screen shot from Research Randomizer listing 595 random numbers between 1 and 71,000

can take time since some of the items may be checked out, and you will have to wait for their return to verify them. Tally the number of errors and calculate an error rate for your catalog. For example, if you found 102 mistakes in your 595 record sample, your error rate is 17 percent. (102/595 = .17) With a confidence interval of four, this can be written as "Between 13 percent and 21 percent of the records in the random sample had errors." This, of course, means that 79 percent to 87 percent of the sample was accurate.

Do you see any patterns to the errors? The 595 records selected are intended for us to make a general estimate of the accuracy of the entire catalog. No catalog will be error free, but looking for a 90 percent accuracy rate is a good goal. In our definition, an error rate is limited to the number of records that were not accurate. The actual number of errors could be much higher, as there could be many mistakes within a single item record.

Conclusion

A statistical sample can indicate in an unbiased fashion the accuracy of the catalog. When this information is presented, the results can help build a case for integrating quality standards in procedures and demonstrate the need for continual monitoring of the collection. In the example library presented, 17 percent of the records and accompanying items were found to be in error. This number may inspire the staff's enthusiasm for accurate procedures and standards. In addition, this method of sampling is a good continuous check on catalog accuracy.

Please note that we haven't used rigorous, exhaustive statistics here. However, for the purposes of our intended audience we can use these general formulas to meet our goal, which is to determine if our library collections warrant a closer look.

John Huber, author of *Lean Library Management*, points out that "What you measure drives performance; therefore, what you do not measure must not be important" and the corollary of that lesson, "What you measure gets most of the attention and therefore drives your priorities" (2011, p.41). In our quest for a holistic library service, we must point out that the metrics we gather should be meaningful to the mission and priorities of the library. We don't gather data just to gather data; we gather data in order to be able to make effective decisions for our organizations. In chapters 4 and 5, as we talk more about how to gather specific data and how to analyze it, keep in mind that what you choose to measure should relate to various service objectives and departments throughout your library.

4

Physical inventory

Abstract: In order to make conclusions about the quality of a collection, the data must be reliable. One way to verify a library collection is to perform a physical inventory. Each physical item is checked against its record as reported by the integrated library system (ILS). This chapter breaks this task into manageable parts, and advocates for integrating inventory into ongoing collection maintenance.

Key words: inventory, internal controls, evaluation, item status, shelf location, item type, RFID, inventory module, physical condition, collection life cycle.

Physical inventory is the act of counting and verifying what is supposedly held by an entity. For a retail business, this is an annual process of reconciliation. It is required by most federal and state authorities in order to accurately calculate the cost of goods sold. Although libraries do not have a profit motive or calculate a cost of goods sold, they do make purchases and have items flow in and out. In many ways, libraries model the behavior of a for-profit entity. In this chapter, we will examine collection inventory as part of a quality control program to verify a library's holdings.

Retail businesses count how much stock was purchased, how much was sold, and how much remains. The number of remaining items for sale gives them the basic profit margin for the business. Keeping a close eye on this margin is the first defense against fraud and theft. It also helps the manager stay focused on the primary performance driver of the business.

This can be illustrated with an example of a retail book business. "Bookstore A" bought 100 copies of a particular title and sold 75. That means 25 should still be in stock, ready for sale. If there are not 25 items left in stock, this difference needs to be explained. Perhaps one or two were damaged in shipping and returned for a refund. Maybe some were stolen. The objective of the inventory is to identify any deviations from the expected process. These explanations help managers make decisions on processes and procedures, not only for efficiency, but to act as a check against fraud and theft.

Libraries may have policies or reporting requirements that call for inventory counts, but for most libraries it is not an obligation. However, this same general inventory technique can help library staff and managers gather good data and keep better track of collections. Regardless of reporting requirements, every library should reconcile the collection purchases they make with their actual holdings as good practice in management and internal controls. This, of course, helps create a quality collection, and ultimately to provide good customer service to library users.

The Department of Library Services at the University of South Africa tested the idea that inventory control has an impact on service quality (Retief and Terblanche, 2006). They measured complaints from library users who could not find what they were looking for, as well as the number of changes they had to make to the library catalog after taking inventory, due to incorrect item records that were found and fixed. They concluded "that the service quality of the library has improved as a result of inventory control" (2006, p.75).

A regular, ongoing practice of tracking collection inventory reduces waste and eliminates redundancy. As with for-profit business entities, internal control of assets is important. For libraries, one of the largest assets is the physical collection of books and other materials. The process of performing a physical inventory provides a periodic check on circulation and purchasing practices, as well as asset reconciliation. When a physical inventory is performed on a library collection, it not only verifies the catalog but also the procedures and processes associated with running a library.

One of the most qualitative uses of physical inventory data is by collection management personnel, who can monitor collection quality. This constant monitoring of the collection by library staff gives a greater hands-on knowledge of the collection. All aspects of library service can improve with this insider knowledge about a collection. Items that have become forgotten or underused can be promoted. Reference skills improve as a result of this intimate knowledge of the collection. Best of all, a regular physical inventory gives an immediate score on how a collection is performing and can help library staff evaluate their collection management processes.

Making physical inventory a regular practice

Businesses perform inventory counts under strict rules. Often, buildings are closed and auditors are hired to manage the process. This is a complicated and often expensive undertaking. Unless a library is mandated by policy, it is not necessary to count inventory at this level of detail. The continual flow of materials both in and out of the building would also make this impractical. Where businesses try to establish a profit margin, a library takes inventory to verify its holdings. Since the objective is different, the process can be less complex.

The mention of "physical inventory" can strike fear into those unfamiliar with the process. First reactions will probably focus on how expensive and time consuming a project like this can be, especially if they are approached with a sales pitch of "counting everything in the library." The sheer number of volumes in even a small library makes inventory seem overwhelming. To put inventory into a perspective that staff can handle, it should be approached on a limited scale, performed continually as part of everyday work, and have limited objectives.

Developing a plan

Initially, one should examine the holdings of a particular collection or a limited part of the collection. The library will need to define some parameters. Perhaps they will begin with the Dewey decimal range of 000–005. Or, they could focus on just the "A"-named authors in fiction. Examining defined pieces of the collection will make the project less overwhelming.

Staff should also brainstorm some issues or problems they would like to address as they go through the inventory process for any given piece of the collection. Here are some example issues that could be addressed while performing an inventory:

■ Correct status of an item: In other words, if an item is checked in, is it where it is supposed to be? Is it marked missing, lost, or damaged in the catalog from a previous error?

- Are items processed into packaging that is appropriate for their type?

- Are the library's most expensive items tracked differently from inexpensive items? For example, are there more checks on an expensive collection like audio books (such as parts counted at both check-in and check-out) than on children's "board books," which are very inexpensive and generally more durable?

- Is there a theft problem, or is there a security system in place for high-theft collections?

Each library's unique history of automation, their current ILS, the shelf arrangement they use, and their staffing needs should be considered in an inventory plan. Let's look at a case study of a library planning its first inventory count. At this particular small public library, initial automation was done by well-meaning, but ill-trained volunteers with no library experience. There was also no consistency or standards applied. At the time the initial automation was done, staff were also ill-trained to correct existing problems in cataloging. Subsequent ILS upgrades and a continued lack of standards compounded the errors. By the time a project to examine the library's holdings was developed, the error rate was so high that there was no clear place to start. Processing and catalog descriptions were so inconsistent that it was difficult for staff to ascertain if certain items listed in the catalog were actually owned by the library at all.

In this public library, a unique history dictated how their inventory project was undertaken. The initial automation was completed in 1995, and then there were at least two additional integrated library systems used before staff began to address their collection problems. For this library, it was imperative to correct the catalog descriptions before attempting to verify holdings. Staff began by using a few minutes a day to go through the shelf list of a defined collection, record by record, and correct the errors. (A further description and discussion of shelf lists follows this section.) They looked at call numbers, serial designations, shelf locations, and item types for each record. This line-by-line attack may seem daunting and time-consuming, but choosing a small piece of the collection at a time helped staff to see results quickly.

At the same time, strict standards for processing and cataloging were firmly established for new items being added to the collection. Going forward, the collection was to have more consistency on the technical services end of the life cycle. This created another boost to the morale of staff that was charged with the catalog clean-up part of the project. The newly organized catalog was to be protected by greater care and more defined standards throughout the collection lifecycle.

Shelf list

A shelf list details all the holdings of a library. If a library has 50,000 items, there should be 50,000 records detailing them. Most ILS programs can generate shelf lists, and usually those lists can be sorted and defined in a variety of ways. The amount of information needed in a shelf list depends on how detailed the inventory project is. If simply verifying holdings, the minimum amount of information needed on a shelf list is:

- Item barcode or identifying number.
- Call number.
- Title.

- Author/Artist.

- Item type (format).

- Shelf location (which collection it is housed in and in a different field from Call Number).

- Status (checked out, missing, checked in, etc.).

- Number of times an item has circulated or been used.

The person performing the inventory uses this information to find the item, and then to reconcile it with the information in its record. (See Figure 4.1.)

Item status is the backbone of a good system, and one of the biggest red flags for identifying collection quality. Is an item checked out, lost, missing, or on the shelf? Accounting for any lag time in shelving, a good ILS will tell you where that material is and what it has been doing, and for how long. Since library materials are constantly in motion, not all items will always be on the shelf. There are many ways to handle this in performing ongoing physical inventory. Specific item holds can be placed on checked-out materials so that upon their return, they will be flagged for an inventory check. Items that the catalog shows to be available on the

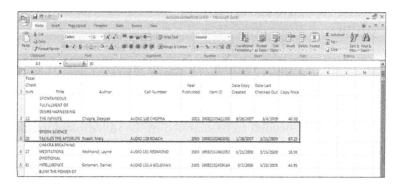

Figure 4.1   Shelf list in an Excel spreadsheet

shelf, but which are not found, can be marked as missing or lost in the catalog and followed up later through other procedures.

It is important to be familiar with the timing aspects of the ILS. If a shelf list for a particular collection is generated first thing in the morning and then used a few hours later, the time lag can affect the reporting of item status. In larger libraries or cooperatives, lag time can even be more than a day or so. The reporting feature of an ILS is not necessarily going to be real time or even close, depending on the system. It is important to keep this in mind when consulting your shelf list. Clarify with your ILS managers on the lag time of report generation and adjust your conclusions accordingly.

It is helpful to think of a shelf list as a picture of the collection at a moment in time. Again, since collections are dynamic, the status of individual items continually changes. New items are added and others are checked out, and still others become lost or missing. Shelf lists have to be dated and managed as to a specific time since they will quickly become obsolete. A good rule of thumb is to only run a defined range of the shelf list; as much as can be handled at once. Run a new, limited-range shelf list every time inventory is worked on so that the data on it reflects the most current activities.

With accurate shelf lists, the actual verification of holdings can begin. At our example library, items were carted up a shelf or two at a time and verified against the fresh shelf list. This library had tagged each item with an RFID system, so the items only needed to be scanned in the inventory module of the ILS. This added a "last inventoried" date to each item. Figures 4.2 and 4.3 show how inventory is taken using two different RFID inventory systems.

Figure 4.2 Handheld RFID inventory equipment

Figure 4.3 Other mobile RFID inventory equipment

What you will discover

Physical inventory reveals many things about a library collection. Laying hands on individual items and looking carefully at each catalog record is a great way to clear up mistakes that are made over time.

Items may be found that are still attached to patron records. They were returned by the patron, but somehow never cleared off of their record. Even the most careful procedures and diligent library staff cannot avoid the occasional slip of an item back to the shelves before being cleared. Physical inventory finds these items and allows staff to clear them. This saves embarrassing confessions by staff to patrons when overdue fines are accrued, but the items were returned on time and found on the shelf.

Items may also be found shelved in the wrong place. Whether staff error or patron browsing is to blame, items find their way to some interesting places on library shelves. A careful look at the items being inventoried will help to find them. They may have been labeled "missing" in the ILS, so be sure to investigate further before re-shelving in the correct location.

Physical inventory also helps identify items that are broken, dirty, or otherwise damaged. When performing the inventory, staff should be diligent about opening covers and flipping quickly through the pages of books. Items should not be inventoried until they are determined to have no loose pages or covers, but in good condition. In audio visual collections, handling cases and discs is the way to assess the number and severity of scratches and the security of discs in the cases. Small pieces break off of cases, allowing discs to slide around inside and become even more scratched. No one wants to check out an item from a library, just to find missing pages or items in an unusable condition (see Figure 4.1).

Figure 4.4   Moldy book found during inventory

Looking carefully at each item record will also help to identify items attached to the wrong record. This requires a trained eye and patience. Records and items may look like a match at first glance, but look at the details carefully. Is an abridgment linked to the unabridged record? For DVDs, is the wide screen edition attached to the full screen record? Is a classic paperback listed as hardcover? Occasionally, one may even find an item that was attached to a record that is completely different, a mistake made by a cataloger at some point. Perhaps someone was linking a stack of items and got distracted, linking each item to the record for the previous item in the stack. Consider this kind of mistake from the patron's perspective. They look up Shakespeare's *Twelfth Night* in the library catalog and are referred by the call number, inexplicably, to the business section of the library. Patrons are confused enough by library classification systems and online catalogs. They don't need another wrinkle in their quest for information.

What about holdings that show up in library catalogs for items that were supposedly discarded ages ago? A shelf list shows a record, but there is no item to be found. It is not checked out and is not marked "missing" or "damaged." It may have been discarded, but its record was never purged. The opposite may also be true: physical inventory may bring an item to hand that is not attached to a record at all, and which may even be clearly labeled "discarded." There is no match on the shelf list, so it seems to be an extra item. There it is, sitting on the shelf, but the record was purged and the item was not.

Public libraries with adult, juvenile, and teen collections add another layer of complexity. Physical inventory may find items in the youth department that are clearly youth materials, but which are labeled as adult (or vice versa). One may also find items that are correctly labeled and correctly cataloged, but which were accidentally shelved in the wrong department. We wouldn't want children stumbling upon adult materials that are inappropriate!

ILS features for inventory

Most of the more sophisticated ILS programs have some type of inventory feature that allows the system to track and follow items that have been inventoried. In most systems, this would be reported in a field of the item record that describes the last time that the item was inventoried. Systematic inventory of collections will indicate the last time any staff member physically examined that item. In conjunction with normal circulation and other quality checks throughout the collection life cycle, an inventory gives the collection and the items a specific marker that a member of staff (meaning a human rather than a computer) actually verified the existence of that particular item. It is important to examine the details of a library's automation system and understand its capabilities and the kinds of data that can be generated.

5

Statistics

Abstract: With reliable data and a verified collection, it is possible to use statistics to make accurate conclusions about the collection. This chapter considers statistics like collection use, age, and turnover. These statistics are put into context like time frame to ensure reliability and accuracy. With accurate statistics, librarians have more tools at their disposal for making decisions about collection management.

Key words: statistics, collection turnover, average age, relative age, collection performance, circulation, last date circulated, ILS, collection currency, collection life cycle.

Once the collection is measured, audited, and inventoried, staff can use the information they have gathered to generate statistics about the library. Now that our catalog data is accurate, we can trust that the statistics we report will also be accurate. Statistics are mathematical calculations that allow the user to make generalized conclusions about large amounts of data. The three basic statistics examined in this chapter will be collection use, age, and turnover. Taken together or separately, these indicators can tell staff a great deal about how the library and its collection perform over time. Decisions can be made regarding selection, weeding, loan policies, and other parts of the collection life cycle. Staff can also use collection statistics in conjunction with other library statistics (such as numbers of reference questions answered or program attendance) to make decisions about staffing requirements and library services offered.

Collection use

One of the most common use statistics is circulation. Libraries with circulating collections will want to measure how many times individual items circulate. (In chapter 3 we discussed what constitutes a "circulation." Here, we will consider a check-out and a check-in as one circulation.) One of the problems with the use of circulation statistics is not putting them into the context of a time frame. Simply stating that something has been checked out 40 times doesn't tell us enough about how that title has really performed. However, if you examine the time frame of when those 40 circulations occurred, you can make some conclusions about the item. Let's consider two items with 40 circulations each.

- Item A has 40 checkouts over the period 1995–2000. No checkouts occurred after 2000.
- Item B has 40 checkouts over the period 2010–2012. Eighty percent of these circulations occurred in 2010.

Although equal in circulations, Item A hasn't budged from the shelf in over a decade. Item B was more popular in 2010, but declined in checkouts in 2011 and 2012. Without the context of a time frame, a circulation statistic is much less useful.

What decisions can we make based on these circulation statistics? An obvious conclusion using the circulation statistic in the example above is weeding. Again, if you just make a weeding decision based on the number of circulations, you may come to the conclusion that an item is popular and should be retained. If Item A really hasn't been checked out in over a decade, it's not that popular any more, and you will want to look at the item more closely for other weeding criteria.

The "last date circulated" statistic is equally misleading taken out of context. Librarians often run reports that list all items in a collection that have not circulated since a certain date. Titles that have circulated more recently than the chosen date are not included on the list. That does not mean that everything that has circulated recently is a good fit for the library's collection. It could be that there is only one item available in a category and patrons have no other choices.

Staffing decisions can also be made using collection statistics. For example, most libraries have fixed staffing budgets. There may be full-time staff and part-time staff, professional staff, paraprofessional staff, and even nonprofessional staff. To schedule staff most efficiently, it is helpful for managers to have statistics on collection use. Most integrated library systems can track how many items were checked out each day, or even each hour of each day. Scheduling staff during the busiest times is important. For example, an academic library may need all hands on deck at the start of a new semester, but fewer during spring break. The various levels of staff of that academic library can be scheduled to match the ebb and flow of library use throughout a semester. At the end of a semester when exams are over, more Pages (staff to re-shelve materials) may be needed to handle the influx of returned materials. At the beginning of the semester, there is probably more going out than coming in. At that time, more reference librarians are necessary to help students find materials for their new coursework, but fewer Pages are necessary. How about a public library with an active summer reading program? More Pages and Circulation staff will be needed to keep the large amounts of materials flowing quickly through the system, but professional staff may be able to concentrate more on activities like presenting programs. Close analysis of collection use will determine what parts of the collection life cycle are the most active at any given time, and managers can schedule staff in those departments accordingly.

Again, using circulation data in conjunction with other statistics is critical. In our holistic view of the library, each department can influence behavior in other areas of the library. At times when a library has a popular program, more staff may be needed for activities like meeting room set-up and clean-up. More specifically, after children's story time, the youth department may need more staff available to help families find and use materials (and to clean up afterward!) and the circulation department may need more staff available to check-out materials. Managers should track the patterns of what is happening throughout the library as a whole, and anticipate staffing needs throughout the building.

Collection age

Collection age is also an important driver of quality. For public and academic libraries, current information is absolutely critical in areas of technology, science, medicine, and law. There are also collection standards based on collection age, such as the Library of Michigan's "Quality Services Audit Checklist." In order to reach the basic level of standards certification, a Michigan public library must "[keep] its collection up-to-date, with a minimum of 15% of its circulating materials acquired within the last five years, and a minimum of 3% of its circulating collection weeded every year" (Library of Michigan, *michigan.gov*).

To determine a collection's age, simply average the publication dates present. Many ILS systems will do this for you, or you can do it in a spreadsheet. Just add up all the publication years and then divide by the number of records present. For example, if you have five publication dates: 2010, 2011, 1999, 2003, and 2002, they add up to 10025. Divide that by five to get the average publication date of these five items: 2005. Now you know that the average age of these five items is the current year minus 2005.

The value of such a number should be used as a guide, and not be considered a standard in itself. It, too, needs to be put into context. Before calculating the average, the data set must be defined and corrected for anything that might give an unfair picture of a collection. For example, let's look at a small public library with about 50,000 physical items in the collection. The first average of all 50,000 publication dates produced an average age of 1987. This can be disturbing to those librarians interested in a current, popular materials collection. However, a closer look at the components of that average age reveals quite a different conclusion.

This particular library had about 5000 items in its local history and genealogy collection. Approximately 10,000 other items were classified as popular fiction, 8000 were nonfiction, and the rest were youth and teen materials. By eliminating the local history and genealogy materials from the calculation, the average age quickly rose about ten years. Yes, the "true" average age of the entire collection was 1987, but that number is somewhat irrelevant in the context of decision making and evaluating the collection. Realistically, each collection should be treated individually and an average age calculated separately. Relative age is not treated equally in all collections. The average age of legal or health collections should be much higher than that of subject areas like classic literature or history.

Average age can be problematic when the range of dates is large. Consider the following seven dates: 1920, 1995, 1999, 2004, 2005, 2006, and 2013. The average date is 1991. The date range is from 1920 to 2013. Given the span of the ages, adjusting your data can give you a truer picture of the average. If we consider the item dated 1920 as a specialty item that really doesn't represent the main collection, and do the average again without the 1920 date, the average age of the six remaining dates is 2003. This example shows that the average age can give a general impression of a collection's age, but one must be observant of the data set. Average age should be used in well-defined groups with an eye toward the actual date range – and the actual items – involved.

Collection turnover

The Library Research Service defines it best: "Turnover rate relates the number of materials checked out relative to the size of the collection. It is the number of materials circulated divided by the number of physical materials held. Turnover rate indicates how often each item in the collection was lent, thus this measure is relevant to use of the collection. It may be useful to compare this figure to selected inputs such as volumes held per capita, and outputs such as circulation per capita and ILLs per 1000 circulation" (Library Research Service, *lrs.org*). Calculating a turnover is useful in evaluating activity.

As with the other statistics, it is essential to work with a well-defined, clean data set. Using specific groups will yield more relevant data. In particular, calculating a turnover rate on the entire collection would not be helpful. Any non-circulating items included in the total collection will under-report turnover, since those items wouldn't circulate anyway. The denominator of this calculation is critical to establishing a turnover. Careful definition of the "total collection" number should be clearly defined and consistently used.

Let's use a sample library and calculate a total collection number for use in a denominator.

Total items reported by the ILS	60,000
Total non-circulating items in reference collection	1000
Total items in non-circulating local history collection	1500
Lost items that are still included in the overall total until resolved	1500
Missing items not yet deleted	1000
Items labeled "damaged"	1000

Calculating a usable total for turnover would be the 60,000 items, less those non-circulating, to bring the net number for the denominator to 54,000 items. There are also other types of inclusions and exclusions to this data set that might aid in analysis. If your ILS includes e-content or periodicals, decisions should be made to include or exclude that number from the denominator.

The numerator in this calculation is also important. We learned how elusive the "circulation" metric can be in chapter 3, but the number of uses needs to be carefully defined and consistently calculated so that comparisons over time are meaningful. As with the denominator, include or exclude those transactions that are most relevant to your analysis. Should ILL transactions be included? Is the turnover significantly different? Should in-house uses be counted? As with the other statistics discussed, there are many variations on this particular calculation. Is the time frame appropriate? Annual, monthly, and quarterly calculations can all present different views of the same data, to be utilized differently depending on the purpose.

Collection turnover, specifically as a tool for collection evaluation, is best used when limited to "like items". In nonfiction, you might break down items based on their Dewey range. In many cases, narrow definitions can yield interesting information. An example might be computer materials. The entire collection of computer materials is 2000, and of that number only 10 items were checked out in the time frame of one year. The turnover of this collection would be calculated as 10/2000, or a rate of 0.005 (which translates into 0.05 percent). This low percentage should immediately flag someone's attention to the choice of computer materials being offered. Were those not circulating out of date? Was a particular publisher or series more popular than others?

The turnover statistic illustrated here is about collection use, but you can also calculate other types of turnover. Turnover measures how much something changes within a scope of time, so this can be applied to staffing, holds/requests to copies, turnaround time to meet ILL requests, and many other library functions.

Putting it together

The real power in these statistics is using them together to assemble an overall picture that will aid in decision-making about the collection and the library as a whole. In proper context, these calculations can help staff make unbiased decisions and flag attention to issues needing further investigation.

These statistics are also good for examining how a collection has changed over time. This is where consistent definitions and reporting will be helpful. Changes in the interests and makeup of a community can be viewed through statistics, allowing the library to respond to changing community needs.

Creating collection objectives and benchmarks

Abstract: Objectives and benchmarks can be used to focus a librarian's goals for a collection. Library vision and mission statements are important in keeping the focus of the library in a general direction. Objectives and benchmarks are practical implementations of that focus. Different libraries will have different users and different missions. Managing a collection should have a specific role in fulfilling a library's mission and vision.

Key words: mission statement, vision statement, selection statement, collection policy, selection policy, objective, benchmark, collection priorities, Dewey Decimal Classification, Library of Congress Classification.

All libraries have limited budgets, space, and time. An objective of collecting everything for everyone is just not possible. Essentially, this means that choices must be made. How those choices get made is where mission statements and collection management policies step in. In this chapter we will describe how vision and mission statements and collection management policies lead to collection objectives, and how the success of those objectives can be tracked through benchmarks. The metrics and statistics previously gathered and analyzed are now put to long-term use and collections are actively managed.

Vision statements and mission statements

Vision statements, according to Gary Hartzell, are not the same as mission statements. His article, "Controlling Your Own Destiny: Why Vision and Mission Statements are Indispensable" describes a vision as "defining the core values and beliefs that drive the organization" (2002, p.37). He says that vision statements are timeless because they define a library's "perpetual purpose" (p.37). The Milwaukee Public Library's vision statement, to give an example, is: "The Milwaukee Public Library is every person's gateway to an expanding world of information. Providing the best in library service, the staff guides Milwaukeeans in their pursuit of knowledge, enjoyment and lifelong learning, ultimately enriching individual lives and the community as a whole" (Milwaukee Public Library, *mpl.org*).

Mission statements give libraries direction. They describe how the organization will achieve that overall purpose described in their vision statement. In public libraries, they often include language about providing materials for the reading and research interests of the community. Milwaukee Public Library's mission statement is "The Milwaukee Public Library provides materials, services and facilities for all citizens of Milwaukee and others in order to meet present and future informational needs and raise the level of civilization in Milwaukee." (Milwaukee Public Library, *mpl.org*). Their vision statement says that they are a gateway to information, and their mission statement indicates what they will provide in order to achieve that vision. Their mission statement may change over time, but their vision is likely to stay the same. Here are a few more example mission statements for public libraries:

The library provides materials and services to help community residents obtain information to meet their personal, educational and professional needs.

The mission of the library is to help community residents meet their personal, educational, and professional information needs.

The function of the library is to provide the people of its community with access to a balanced collection of books and other materials which will serve their educational, cultural, and recreational needs.

In an academic library, mission statements may guide the library to support the research and curriculum needs of students and faculty. Some academic library mission statements include:

The library's mission is to support the research needs and enhance the information literacy skills of students, faculty, and staff.

The mission of the library is to provide the collections, services, and environments to support the teaching, learning, and research needs of the university.

The library's mission is to provide resources, services, and gateways to information to meet the needs of the university's instructional, research, and outreach programs.

Betty Carter's article, "Leading Forward by Looking Backward" says that the mission statement is the "backbone of your program" (2007, p.16). She continues with, "Each kind of statement speaks to the kinds and numbers of materials librarians will have in their collections" (p.16). Her example is school libraries, but her ideas apply to any kind of library. If the library's purpose is to support research interests, its collection is likely to be largely made up of scholarly and intellectual materials. If its purpose is to meet cultural and recreation needs, its collection probably has more popular and mainstream materials.

Carter also says that, "The mission statements of both an individual school and the district in which it resides should be a part of your collection development plan" (2007, p.17). Again, this could apply to various libraries on a college campus or various branches of a public library system. If the larger entity (the "headquarters" of the library system) has a mission for the system as a whole, each individual library should consider how that mission fits into its own collection management policy, and even consider writing its own mission statement that complements and expands upon the other. This will allow each library to collect materials to meet its individual users' needs. For example, a university science library may find it valuable to create its own mission statement that indicates its support of science research specifically, but that mission statement is clearly still related to the university library system's mission to "support the research needs of faculty and students." Having its own mission points the science library's collection management policy to specifically science materials. The mission statement, then, is the starting point of collection quality, and leads to the collection management policy.

Collection management policies

In our first chapter, we described how collection management policies are the foundation of a quality collection. In this chapter, we take that idea one step further to show how mission statements, collection management policies, collection objectives, and benchmarks are related in a holistic library environment.

Where a mission statement gives the library direction, its collection management policy articulates that mission with respect to the collection. In the era before multiple formats, a collection management policy simply articulated what kind of books the library would purchase. In modern libraries, the variety of formats and items available require management to define the scope of the collection. Collection management policies also provide some protection against overt censorship, particular social and political agendas, as well as carry out the library's mission.

Libraries may have what they call "selection statements" or even "materials selection policies" that describe, in a paragraph or two, the general scope of the collection. The difference is that collection management policies provide more detail for each of the library's collections and include other collection management activities besides selection (such as how weeding will be carried out and how gifts and donations will be handled). A selection statement indicates what the library intends to collect. A collection management policy binds the library to deliver what was intended in each area in which it collects and to carry out all other responsibilities related to managing a collection. Another way to phrase it would be to create a document called "collection management guidelines." This is more of an internal document that collection managers can refer to when the library does not wish to create an official policy.

Again, we highly recommend that a formal policy be written, endorsed by the library's Board of Trustees, and is made available to staff and library users that highlights criteria for decision-making throughout the collection life cycle.

Let's use the example of a public library audio-book collection. The library's collection management policy has an adult audio-book section that states:

> The primary purpose for purchasing audio books is to provide public access to spoken recordings of print material. This will include, but not be limited to, unabridged works of fiction, non-fiction, poetry, drama, foreign language instruction, and self-improvement or instructional material. Criteria to be considered include:
>
> - physical quality of format
> - reputation of the vendor and replacement policies
> - performance quality
> - popularly accepted formats
> - cost related to estimated patron use.

Notice that this particular library did not indicate a specific format; only that it would collect "spoken recordings of print material." This leaves room for the selectors of this collection to adapt to changing technologies without having to change the collection policy.

In another example, a community college defines its collection in terms of curriculum. Again, the language used is broad and points toward its mission of education. In this particular example, the college uses faculty input as a primary criterion for the media collection:

> The purpose of the media collection is to support the instruction and research needs of the faculty and students. The collection supports present and future

teaching needs in all fields of study offered at [College]. Emphasis is placed on faculty requests in support of the curriculum.

The variety of collection management policies and examples are too numerous for the purposes of this book. For this chapter, suffice it to say that collection management policies and selection statements are unique to the libraries they serve, and selectors should use them as guideposts for collection management decisions throughout the collection lifecycle.

Collection objectives

The library's mission describes its overall purpose. Its collection management policy defines what types of things it will collect, and for whom, how those items will be managed throughout the collection life cycle, and it outlines how the collection will contribute to the library's mission. Collection objectives are the next level of detail. They dictate what the librarian is hoping to accomplish with each collection and state criteria for selection.

Returning to our audio book example, the selector is most concerned with getting a maximum amount of uses for the money spent to acquire them. The selector has determined that popular fiction titles from bestseller lists and classic titles that have continual demand would be the most appropriate choices for the library's audio book collection. In consideration of nonfiction titles, the selector has determined that foreign language instruction and popular nonfiction titles would be also appropriate. Travel, medical, and legal information, which have a limited shelf life due to the need for currency in those collections, will be de-emphasized.

For our audio book example, the following collection objectives have been established:

- Select current fiction titles that are unabridged.

- Select popular and current nonfiction titles that are unabridged.

- Select classic titles which continually have demand.

- Only purchase the CD format. (Objectives, unlike policies that have to be approved by a governing board, can be updated easily as new formats become available or are demanded by the public.)

- Give lower priority to series fiction to limit commitments to future purchases.

- Give lower priority to non-fiction titles that might become outdated or irrelevant quickly.

Right away, policy and objectives are easily differentiated. Policy is a framework; a somewhat static document taking a long view of the collection. Objectives are current and can quickly adapt to changes in technology, popularity, and community interests. Collection objectives are not a formal statement of policy, but provide some criteria to help the selector. This can also be a tool for supervisors to manage the selectors they oversee. Collection objectives are more about results than process.

What parts of the collection should have collection objectives? This is going to be driven by how the collection is organized and how responsibilities of selection are divided by staff. In a public library that has separate collections for mystery, science fiction, and other genres, separate collection objectives might be written if there are distinct differences in the expectations of these collections. If the same objectives are appropriate for similar collections, then create objectives for the entire group. In general, objectives should be written whenever there is something specific for the selector to consider or manage, and should be driven by the collection's particular needs.

To give another example, in a public library's youth collection the selectors have decided to have a small collection of paperback books that have an average cost of two dollars per unit. It is expected that these paperbacks will not last long in terms of condition. Contrast this to a youth video game collection with a unit cost of around thirty dollars. The higher unit cost demands that selectors watch the performance of this collection closely. Appropriate objectives will depend on the type and goal of the collection, and because not all collections are created equally, objectives should also be tailored to reflect those differences.

Creating collection objectives is also useful when creating a new collection within the library. Perhaps through some budget management, and rearrangement of materials, a library decides to launch a separate section for science fiction. Setting collection objectives prior to creating the collection will help the selectors choose materials (and spaces, cataloging rules, etc.) for the collection. Will the collection be made up of paperbacks? Series? An emphasis on newly published titles vs. classic science fiction? These are all objectives to include.

In academic libraries, more collection objectives may be necessary. Accreditation issues could be incorporated into the objectives. The difference in use between students and faculty should also be considered. They may give higher priority to texts in the areas of faculty research interests and less to popular, "bestseller" fiction and nonfiction.

Modern library management, as well as the fiscal responsibility of selectors, requires them to pay close attention to the library's mission statement, collection policy, and collection objectives. They must articulate the purpose of the collection to both management and users. This means making difficult choices in formats and titles. Setting priorities can be difficult. Changing technology and access to information presents many challenges to selectors to get the most for their users – within budgetary and space guidelines.

Creating benchmarks

A benchmark is a standard by which a collection can be measured or judged. Libraries can set benchmarks to determine how well their collections perform within a variety of criteria. One of the most common benchmarks in libraries is the number of circulations, or uses, of items in a collection. Comparing a library's performance to another similar library is one way to create benchmarks. Analysis of the circulation trend of a particular collection from year to year is another way to benchmark. For the purposes of this discussion there are two kinds of benchmarking: external and internal.

External benchmarking measures a library's performance to a similar library or a library in a similar community. It is helpful to measure against a library that has a similar budget, population, staff, and/or collection size. However, with any of these general guidelines, benchmarking against another library's data can only be taken so far. Many factors contribute to the overall performance of a library, and the collection is only one factor. Staffing, management, and philosophy of service can vary greatly even between demographically or financially similar libraries. External benchmarks can reveal overall generalized performance measures, but are not helpful in measuring specific collection performance. Even if similar criteria and collections are used, the difference in things like building hours and circulation policies could negate some conclusions made about the collection's performance.

Internal benchmarking is more helpful to library staff in discussing quality collections and performance. A collection is defined and measured against a standard. This "apples to apples" context will indicate how a collection is performing against itself rather than other collections with different objectives. Benchmarks allow library staff to determine if items in a collection are popular with library users and being used as intended. For an internal benchmark, a library sets an expectation for a collection and then follows data to see if the collection is performing as expected.

Let's use an example that illustrates how this is accomplished. A public librarian wants to begin a collection of graphic novels targeted at teens. The library has determined that this collection will support its mission, and the collection has been added to the collection management policy. The collection objective states that the collection will focus on popular, mainstream, and award winning titles that are bound as books (not individual comic magazines), and intended for ages thirteen to eighteen. A budget has been set and a base collection of titles has been selected. A marketing plan is prepared, and processing and shelving of the collection have also been considered. The books are on the shelf and ready to be checked out. Benchmarks now need to be set to let the staff know if their idea for this new collection was successful.

In order to set benchmarks, staff began by finding out what other libraries in the area had graphic novels collections. Then they simply asked the staff of those libraries how their collections were being received by teens. A neighboring library said that teen graphic novels were "very popular" after a good display and a lot of promotion. Since each staff member might have a different idea of what constitutes popularity, a conservative estimate can be made based on the maximum possible circulations in a three month period (assuming no renewals and that items are returned to the library on their assigned due dates but not before). For our example library, graphic novels circulate for one month at a time. Their maximum use in three months, with our criteria, is three circulations. The benchmark for this new collection will be set at three circulations within three months of being added to the collection. This is the performance that the library is striving to achieve with this collection.

This benchmark can be analyzed in a variety of ways in order to judge the success of the collection. Staff should find out how many or what percentage of items in the collection did not reach the benchmark, as well as what percentage of the collection did. Additional information can also be used in this context. What about the next three months, and after a year has passed? It is also possible to track what authors, titles, and series generated more or fewer circulations compared to others. The point of this example is to start by setting the benchmark and then judge the merits of the collection against that standard.

Again, circulation is not the only quality marker for a collection. In a medical collection or reference collection, for example, currency is an important issue. Creating a benchmark of an average age of a collection is also useful in measuring quality. For example, a medical collection benchmark could state that the average age of the collection be five years. Every three to six months a shelf list is analyzed by publication dates and an average is calculated.

Depending on the collection, each subject matter or item type has a particular driving issue that defines it as a quality collection. For a popular fiction collection, circulation will be a driving factor. For medical or legal reference, currency is a compelling factor. In literature and the arts, currency is not as much a concern as preservation or breadth of subject matter. Identifying a collection's quality driver is where one begins in creating a benchmark.

The classification system in place at any library creates a natural starting point for creating benchmarks. Take the example of a medium sized public library using the Dewey Decimal System, which has separate collections for career materials and biographies, shelved apart from the rest of the nonfiction collection. Within the Dewey Decimal ranges for any collections, benchmarks can be developed. This library uses the following Dewey Decimal breakdowns:

000	Generalities
100	Philosophy & psychology
200	Religion
300	Social sciences
400	Language
500	Natural sciences & mathematics
600	Technology (Applied sciences)
700	The arts
800	Literature & rhetoric
900	Geography & history

Biography (921)

Careers (selected 650's and other appropriate materials from other Dewey ranges)

Of course, each Dewey range listed above has to divide individual subject collections internally for benchmarking. For example, computer materials (from within the 000 range) should not have the same benchmarks as bibliographies (also from within the 000 range). Each Dewey range should break into sub-collections for the purposes of setting benchmarks of performance, selection, and de-selection.

This is probably best illustrated using a large group like the 600's. Although the general term is "technology," we are really dealing with many subjects that require very different treatment for the purposes of collection management. At the beginning of the 600's, there is a catch-all, general group of materials that deals with technology. Medical materials encompass the 610's, and although the number range itself is small (610–619), a great deal of medical subjects are included within that range. This particular group should have its own benchmarks. Depending on budgets and staffing available, these sections could be subdivided even further. Does a medical dictionary have the same criteria as a handbook on current medications or medical testing? Even though they are items that make up the same collection, a dictionary might remain valid longer than a handbook, or garner more (or fewer) uses. Further down the 600's range are pets, gardening, and other home arts that may not share the issues defined in the medical category, and therefore require different benchmarks.

In a large academic library that uses Library of Congress classification, conspectus subject categories could be used to break down the subdivisions for objectives and benchmarks. An article by Knievel, Wicht, and Connaway defines conspectus subject categories as "broad subject classifications based on the Library of Congress classification system that provide a basis for large research libraries to assess the subject distribution of their collections. The conspectus classification has twenty-five subject areas" (2006, p.39). (See Figure 6.1.)

Creating the benchmarks from scratch is not as overwhelming as it might appear. In our example of how many circulations a new graphic novel would need to constitute a "good" or "smart" purchase, we estimated three checkouts within the first three months. Other popular

1	Agriculture
2	Anthropology
3	Art and architecture
4	Biological sciences
5	Business and economics
6	Chemistry
7	Computer science
8	Education
9	Engineering and technology
10	Geography and earth sciences
11	History and auxiliary sciences
12	Invalid or unknown
13	Language, linguistics and literature
14	Law
15	Library science, generalities and reference
16	Mathematics
17	Medicine
18	Music
19	Performing arts
20	Philosophy and religion
21	Physical education and recreation
22	Physical sciences
23	Political science
24	Psychology
25	Sociology

Figure 6.1 Conspectus subject categories

materials would probably benefit from a similar type of benchmark. Bestselling fiction and nonfiction behave in many of the same ways as a new graphic-novels collection in terms of popularity and wait listing. Those items in the nonfiction collection purchased to replace older items or fill a gap in a subject area should have a completely different benchmark than popular bestsellers. These materials might set a checkout standard that covers its entire life span, or maybe a certain number of checkouts per year.

Here is another example: A public library's new fiction collection has a policy of purchasing popular titles for the community it serves. There is an objective of limiting patron wait time for bestsellers. The library in question also wants to maximize the number of checkouts on each copy. In this example, two opportunities for measuring performance of the collection are available: the number of circulations per volume and the number of holds, or the expected wait time, per copy. Most ILS systems can generate this data. Through past experience, the library staff has determined that three to four checkouts within six months of purchase is a good benchmark for popular fiction.

The key to making effective benchmarks is that expectations of circulation or currency are not going to be fixed across all subjects or genres. A feature film DVD does not have the same performance expectation as a child's picture book. Different age group targets, collection types, and formats all have different performance standards within a library's collection. Grouping like items or subjects together to create performance benchmarks assures appropriate data collection and gives library staff an "apples to apples" comparison.

Holistic benchmarking: overall collection performance

We have seen how subdividing and separating collections is essential for setting objectives and benchmarks, but it is also important to look at a library's combined collections as a whole entity so that a more global analysis can be performed. More holistic, all-encompassing benchmarks measure overall collection performance. For most libraries, circulation figures are the core statistic gathered and used. As mentioned earlier, comparing two separate libraries – although interesting – is not necessarily helpful in creating an overall performance benchmark. However, as we stated in the previous chapter about statistics, circulation figures, used in conjunction with other statistics, can help libraries evaluate how they are serving their users.

Collection organization

Abstract: The physical building and space are the primary drivers of collection organization. A building with multiple floors has different considerations than a library on one level. In addition, the building floor plan is important. Collections need to be user friendly, workflows of staff need to be considered, and also the variety of formats in library collections. Other collection organizational strategies include allocating appropriate shelf space and the use of alternative classification systems.

Key words: physical space, building layout, floor plan, shelving, ergonomics, interfiling formats, BISAC, Dewey Decimal System, neighborhood collections, signage.

This chapter considers how the physical layout of a library's collections contributes to collection quality. Some of the implications in this area impact on physical space, such as building layout, floor plan, and shelving, as well as classification systems, ergonomics, and signage. We will also discuss how the physical layout of staff work areas contributes to collection quality. This expands on our previous discussion of workflow efficiency, but with more emphasis on physical spaces.

Physical space

Building layout is the first consideration in a discussion of a library's physical space. When staff decide where to house a collection, they need to make sense of the functionality of each part of the building. Let's look at an example of a public library that is situated on three floors. The lower level is designated for youth materials, the street level for popular materials like fiction, bestsellers, and A/V collections, and the upper level for research materials like nonfiction, business, and reference collections. A quality collection in this example is dependent on these definitions. This library chose to place children's research materials with the children's collection, rather than on the upper level with the nonfiction and reference materials. This library defines its youth collections first by age level (which determines that it does belong on the lower level) and then by purpose. On the lower level in the youth area, nonfiction and reference materials have their own shelving areas. Each title is defined clearly in the library catalog as juvenile nonfiction or juvenile reference. In this example, the function of the lower level of the building is determined by the materials housed there: those for youth. This library has decided that the function of each floor of its building is directly related to the users of the collections housed there. It would not make sense for this library to have youth materials on all three floors; they have assigned one physical space in the building specifically for children.

What about a technology-centered collection like CD-ROMs or video console games? Staff must consider the goal of the collection and match it with the purpose of the place in which it is housed. Are the games for children? Are they educational games? Are they adult software programs like language learning? The answers to these questions determine the best place to shelve them. Quality collections are achieved when there is harmony between its users and the space it occupies.

A library's floor plan is another consideration. Not only the building layout – which could range from a one-room school library to a multi-wing academic library – but also the way each space is laid out. Are there load-bearing pillars in the middle of the room that shelving must be organized around? Are there architectural features like built-in benches, arches, or windows that break the continuity of the shelving? When deciding where to place each collection, space planners should try to keep collections together. For example, a quality collection would have a continuous run of audio books or DVDs. If the shelving runs out in the middle of the collection and the next available shelf is out of sight (around a corner or behind a pillar), a different space should be found for that collection. Staff should take into consideration how many items are in a collection and how many of those items are typically available at any given time (not checked out) before deciding how many shelves it will require.

Logically dividing collections will help to ensure that shelf space is available. Public libraries may want to separate mystery from fiction or audio books from print books. Academic libraries may need to pull out special collections like English as a Second Language or maps to make more space in the regular Library of Congress classification ranges. Special libraries like archives and museums need to take special care to make sure that delicate items have appropriate holding places that will not damage the items, and which preserve them.

On a related note, placing collections near other similar collections may benefit library users. For example, public libraries may purchase titles in various formats: audio, large print, hardcover, paperback, and/or DVD. Depending on the floor plan of the library, they have to choose if formats will be interfiled so that library users see all of the available options in one place, or if the formats will be shelved separately. Separate shelving might be great for browsers who are just looking for a good audio book. However, interfiled formats might increase circulation simply because library users see what is available in one place. They don't have to check three or four separate collections around the library for a specific title. Patrons may only check the shelf in the one collection they are familiar with and not even consider looking in other places for the same title in a different format. Staff need to consider how much space is available for any given format, and in which spaces around the room, so that if they choose to separate collections, logical divisions are made in shelving.

When deciding how much shelf space to devote to a collection, its popularity with library users is another way to work out shelving needs. Tony Greiner's article, "Collection Development and Shelf Space: A Proposal for Nonfiction Collections" says that "the amount of shelf space allocated to different parts of the collection affects use" (2005, p.347). He suggests that more shelf space needs to be devoted to popular parts of the collection. Library users will find more items on topics they want because the library will have more space devoted to those topics. Shifting collections as they go in and out of fashion, and as weeding is performed, will keep open shelving for the most used collections. Greiner suggests a detailed formula to figure out how much space should be allocated to each piece of the collection, including data like available shelving, number of items in the collection, and circulation figures.

The Plymouth (Michigan) District Library (PDL) took his advice, and in the summer of 2011 balanced the shelves of their adult nonfiction collection. In this library, the entire range of adult nonfiction is located in a contiguous area of shelving. There are thirteen two-sided rows where nonfiction titles are shelved in Dewey decimal order from 000 through 999. Over years of collection maintenance, some areas of this collection became very full, while others were heavily weeded. For example, sections like the 700s (fine arts) and the 900s (history) were maintained for demand and condition, but grew in size. Other more time-sensitive sections like the 610s (health), the 332s (personal finance), and the 004s (computers) were maintained more for currency and relevancy. Those sections stayed roughly the same in terms of total numbers of volumes. As titles were weeded, new titles were added at about the same rate. Yet other sections, like the 800s (literature), were heavily weeded of large, multi-volume series that were replaced with digital copies, creating large pockets of shelf space. The library followed Greiner's formula to balance the available shelving with the current space needs of the nonfiction collection. This huge, physical shifting does not need to be undertaken very often (maybe every five to ten years, depending on the library), but it made a huge difference to the browsability of PDL's collection. The library was able to create plenty of space for collections that needed it, while also planning for future purchases and growth in popular subject areas.

Classification systems

There is a recent trend in public libraries of using a book store arrangement to shelve materials instead of a traditional Dewey Decimal System. According to Sarah Hopkins, author of "Decimating Dewey: Introducing a Bookshop Arrangement for Shelving the Nonfiction Collection," a Dewey arrangement "does not facilitate browsing in the areas of most interest to public library users" (2007, p.8). By taking popular subjects and grouping them together in a more browsable, eye-catching way, nonfiction circulates better. It also helps library users avoid frustration and information overload, and saves them time.

This is supported in "The Dewey Dilemma," an article written by Barbara Fister (2009). "Browsability" is her goal for library collections that are organized using the book industry's BISAC system (p.22). She describes how the BISAC system uses an alphabetical list of categories to arrange collections. She believes that switching from Dewey to this simple, user-friendly system in libraries helps library users to be more self-sufficient in finding materials. She quotes patrons saying [about the Dewey Decimal System], "those numbers scare me," "I don't understand them," and "they make me feel stupid" (p.22).

The Plymouth District Library, highlighted above, has created what they call "neighborhoods." They chose a few popular nonfiction collections and pulled them out from the regular Dewey decimal arrangement. There are browsing collections – neighborhoods – on cooking, home improvement, crafts, gardening, travel, ESL, exam/test prep, job search, college search, and genealogy. Librarians decided what materials belonged in these categories. For example, the gardening collection pulled materials from gardening (635 in the Dewey system) and landscaping (712 in the Dewey system). Patrons looking for information on gardening will now find similar materials all in one place, rather than having to track down two separate call numbers. The downside to this physical arrangement is that these featured collections are physically separated from the rest of the nonfiction collection. The regular Dewey decimal ranges are in a row on one side of the room, while the featured collections begin on an adjoining wall and wrap around the next corner. Patrons often do not know to look in a different physical area of the library for books shelved in "neighborhood" collections. Even though the library catalog clearly states "Gardening Collection – Upper Level," it also gives a Dewey decimal call number. Within the gardening collection, the materials are still arranged by Dewey. Many people disregard the "Gardening Collection" notation and go straight to the call number area of the regular nonfiction stacks. (See Figures 7.1 and 7.2.)

Shonda Brisco disagrees with the idea of libraries using bookstore arrangements. Her article, "Dewey or Dalton?" indicates that libraries are better than bookstores because they have a system, and that system is universal between libraries (2004). A customer who walks into a bookstore has to figure out that bookstore's arrangement, but nonfiction books will always have the same number in any library that uses the Dewey Decimal System.

Figure 7.1   "Neighborhood" browsing collections in a public library

Figure 7.2 Sign for browsing collections, or "neighborhoods"

Regardless of the organization a library chooses, a quality collection has a classification system that users understand and that helps them find what they want on the shelves.

Ergonomics

Ergonomics has to do with how workers interact with their work environment. Here, we are concerned with how library users and staff interact with library collections. Movement impacts collections in terms of wear and tear and shelving accuracy, and impacts staff in terms of bodily stress. A quality collection is handled efficiently on both counts.

First, let's consider formats. There are a variety of cases, wrappings, and other storage options for library materials. For example, many libraries choose to keep their AV collections in locking cases. These cases must be unlocked before they can be used and locked before they are re-shelved. Depending on the type of case, staff must engage and disengage some sort of locking mechanism. The more times the case is locked and unlocked, the more wear and tear on the case, the lock, and even the staff person. In another example, audio books with a large number of discs may be placed in very large cases that can accommodate more discs. These large cases may be heavier, bulkier, and more awkward for staff to work with. Every time the audio book is checked out, staff members will want to count the discs to make sure they are all there. Every time the audio book is returned, they will count the parts again. In fact, every time a patron switches to the next disc, the case will have to be opened (20 discs equals 20 openings and closings of the case!). Again, depending on the case, all of these openings and closings may cause the case to break down (not to mention the user's hands!). Libraries should consider all the possible options when choosing cases to process their materials into. Perhaps there is a format that requires fewer openings and closings, or maybe there is machinery that can do it for staff automatically. With RFID, there are automatic lockers and unlockers that cases can be slipped into easily.

Shelving and circulation both have a lot of implications for ergonomics, which were mentioned in chapter 2. The more complicated a workflow, the less ergonomic it may be. Any staff who handle carts and materials should look carefully at their workflows for ergonomic efficiency. Medicine Hat Library in Alberta, Canada set up an ergonomics committee to look closely at the ergonomic efficiency of various workflows in their building (Fraser and Munro, 2004). They examined what they call the "work triangle" and found that their check-in procedure had "unnecessary handling and carrying of the books, adding to the stresses on the back and upper limbs" (p. 234). They also found that the laser pens they used to read barcodes at check-out and check-in required pinch grips that stressed tendons of the hands. They looked for a solution that would read barcodes when books were moved under/over them (p. 237). The quality of a collection is affected by ergonomics, and Medicine Hat Library changed their physical spaces and their workflows to help the situation. When materials are easier to handle and more efficiently moved from place to place, the quality of the collection improves.

To take this example a little further, let's talk about the layout of staff workspace. In a technical services area where books are received, processed, cataloged, linked, and then taken out for shelving, the best staff set-up would follow that life cycle chronologically. The materials would be passed from one area to the next as each step is completed. This would cut down on how often and how far the materials are transferred from one area to the next. Imagine if some of those processes took place on a different floor of a building or even at different ends of the room. Items would have to be carted up more times and it would take longer to complete the full circuit to make the materials available to library users.

Another example of this could be in circulation processes. Book return bins must be emptied and the items transferred to the place where "discharging" or "checking-in" happens (removing items from user accounts). Various processes happen at the check-in phase, such as counting parts, checking for damages, and filling new holds on returned items. Anything that happens as part of the check-in workflow should be able to be taken care of in that same physical space. It doesn't make sense to cart items up from a book return bin, transfer them to another area of the library, unload the cart, handle them in various ways during discharge, cart them up again either for shelving or for moving them to the patron holds area.

Physical spaces in staff areas are as important to collection quality as the spaces for the materials themselves. The more ergonomically materials are handled by staff, the more available and usable they are for library patrons.

Signage

Signage is a catch-22 for libraries. Not enough signs and your patrons don't have enough information to find what they are looking for, whether that is a restroom or a library collection. Too many signs and they are overwhelmed by information overload. Signage has an important effect on collection quality. It affects access and use, which are crucial to the success of most libraries.

Consider a library that serves speakers of a different language. If the patron's first language is not that of the library community, those patrons may feel isolated and frustrated when they come to the library. Imagine not being able to read the sign that designates the English as a Second Language collection! Libraries that serve a high population of patrons that speak certain languages should consider posting their signs in those languages. Even visual clues on signage will help these patrons (Schmidt and Wilson, 1998). What if a library had a collection of books in Spanish, but the Spanish-speakers didn't understand the English sign that reads "Books in Spanish?" In these examples, the collections intended for non-native speakers might not be used because the intended audience can't find them.

121

Children are another group of library users that need special signage. Small children who can't yet read, or who are just learning to read, should be given picture clues to help them find items in the library. Sure, their parents probably help them find specific titles, but children will be more comfortable in the library, and learn about its services and how to use it at a younger age and more easily with signage they can recognize. Youth signage needs to be lower, bigger, and brighter. Signage they can understand will also help children put these items back in the right place when they are finished. (See Figure 7.3.)

Signs that announce collections and collection rules (such as "Reference materials do not circulate") also need to be big enough for library users to read. Can low vision patrons read the sign for a large print collection? Can they see it from far enough away to be useful? Low vision patrons may need signage that is not only bigger, but in different colors. Some people see light font on dark background better than the reverse. Some see yellow easier than white. Some see signs

Figure 7.3   Signage with good visual clue

that are directly lit better than those in shadow. Some see slightly dull signs easier than the glare of direct light. There are standards for the average person, spelled out by the Association of Research Libraries at *arl.org*, but for special collections specifically for low vision users, care should be taken in signage so that access is improved (Ragsdale and Kenney, 1995).

Signage that uses "library words" is among the least affective. Do library users know what words like "reference," "circulation," and "nonfiction" mean? In order to be truly useful, signs need to use words that the general public understands. Alternatives to these library words could be, "for library use only," "check out," and "informational." When the sign says "Reader's Advisory," and the patron wants advice on what book will help them fix their car, is it their fault that they didn't go to the "Reference" desk instead? They wanted advice on what book to read to learn how to fix their car: reader's advisory. (See Figures 7.4 and 7.5.) Library lingo means nothing to the public, so it should not be used on signs meant for them. Asking questions of the wrong librarian at the wrong desk is

Figure 7.4   Signage with library jargon

Figure 7.5   Signage with layperson words

frustrating, and ultimately leads to a customer service debacle if not handled carefully by the staff person. It is not up to the patron to know what they can ask of whom. Even handled gracefully, it is a time-waster for the patron to have to ask again at a different desk, or to spend time figuring out what a sign means. The Association of Research Libraries' (1995) "Effective Library Signage" flyer notes, "The signs in a library building set the stage for a friendly or a hostile environment, for a helpful or confusing library visit, especially for first-time users" (Ragsdale and Kenney, 1995).

Displays

Displays are a great way to use physical space to help people use collections and boost their popularity. Rosey Clark's article "Impact Library Access with Bold Use of Color and Space" suggests, "Book displays of out-facing books create excitement about the items in your collection" (2008, p.17). Certainly, a collection of quality should be exhibited, showed off, and even flaunted! Clark suggests making miniature displays at the end of various shelves so that there are outward-facing titles here and there throughout the collection itself. This does not require any extra display furniture, and nicely reveals some of the gems within the collection. Displays that are separate from the collections from which they came could actually confuse library users. They might get excited about the topics and titles exhibited and want to browse what else the library has on those subjects, but since the display is nowhere near the actual shelving location they may have trouble finding more. Displaying the books right on their shelves gives an appealing bookstore feel, but leaves the books near their correct shelving locations. (See Figures 7.6 and 7.7.)

Figure 7.6 Books displayed within the collection they are shelved in

Figure 7.7 Front-faced shelving installed within a collection to display books there

Conclusion

Physical spaces determine how library users experience the collection. If they see a well cared-for building that is attractive on the outside and walk into an inviting, comfortable environment on the inside, they are likely to stay longer and come back more often. When the physical space helps people use the collections, the collection gains quality. Equally, when library materials are classified in a way that users can find what they need quickly and easily, the collection also improves.

Collection budgets

Abstract: All libraries must work within the constraints of available resources. No library has unlimited space or funding. Controlling costs is essential. Many libraries outsource processing, selection, and other parts of the lifecycle as a response to these limits. Donations, grants, and other alternative funding sources should be included in budgeting strategies.

Key words: budget, item cost, affiliate program, outsourcing, negotiation, group discount, fundraising,, book sale, interlibrary loan, collection philosophy.

In tough economic times, libraries have to tighten their budgets. A 2009 survey by *Library Journal* revealed that the biggest challenge to libraries was rising materials prices, followed by escalating energy costs and the increasing demand for services and programs (Oder, 2009, pp.32–3). The survey also revealed that many libraries expected materials budgets to decline. Combined with the increased cost of materials and rising demand for new media, this means that libraries have to do more with less.

There are many factors that affect library collection budgets. Each part of the collection life cycle has an implication for budgeting. The purpose of this chapter is to suggest practical ways that libraries can save money in their budgets without affecting the quality of their collections.

Vendors, deals, donation programs, formats, and collection philosophy all come into play. This chapter assumes a line item budget; our next chapter will introduce the idea of a holistic "program budget."

Vendors

Previously, it was pointed out that relationships with vendors are important to smooth transactions. Generally, libraries have preferred sellers for collection materials. These are companies that often specialize in libraries and understand library missions and services. They have special replacement programs, return guidelines, and sometimes shipping and handling policies.

One way to maximize a materials budget is to look for affiliate programs. In some cases, connecting to online stores through special web links will result in compensation for the library. The library becomes an affiliate, usually with a special corporate account with the vendor, and simply links to the vendor's online store through a specific URL. The vendor either applies discounts to the shopper's bill or gives them a commission for shopping with them. The commission could be in the form of a check paid to the library regularly or a credit to their affiliate account for future shopping. This is a great way for libraries to save money. They are probably shopping with the vendor anyway, and the affiliate account provides them with more money to spend on library materials. It's free money! This particular strategy impacts the quality of the collection in a positive way because it allows the library to purchase more materials than they could have without the extra money coming in.

Another way to maximize a collection budget is a bit more controversial, and has more potential to affect the quality of the collection. A fairly new tactic that some libraries have tried is to hand over selection and processing of materials to the vendors. Proponents of this idea say that it saves staff time in areas like reading review journals, compiling orders, and physically processing items, as well as stocking and paying for processing materials. This model "[shifts] the library focus to public service," according to Barbara Hoffert's article, "Who's Selecting Now?" (2007, p.40). Hoffert describes the Phoenix Public Library's decision to hand over selection of library materials to its vendors. Phoenix staff found that about 80 percent of their collection choices were the results of standing orders and titles that were not reviewed. The majority of what they were buying was from vendor-generated lists and vendor suggestions. Hence, they decided to have the selectors spend their time reviewing the vendors' lists and analyzing the vendor-selection service. Some vendors do charge a per-item cost or decrease the discount they would normally provide for the value-added service of doing the selecting for the library. The cost savings, then, are primarily in staffing and time. Collection managers are freed up for more work in other areas of collection managing: promoting use, bibliographic instruction, and weeding. The library may also save money on review journal subscriptions that they no longer need.

Outsourcing the processing of library materials is another potential area for cost savings. The library can devote the staff and the space formerly used for processing to another endeavor. They can also re-assign the money formerly spent on processing materials like labels, stickers, cases, and book covers, as well as the equipment used in processing.

A less drastic (and less controversial) method of maximizing collection budgets and staff time can be achieved through standing orders. Libraries can set up standing orders for many types of materials. Vendors receive a set of criteria for library materials and fill orders automatically based on those conditions. For example, a public library could set up a standing order for a particular series of travel books. Every time a new travel guide is published in that series, the library automatically receives a copy. Most standing orders can be even more specific. The library could specify that every time a travel guide for a specific place is published in that series, they automatically receive a copy. This frees librarians from having to keep up with the new releases. They know they will purchase the title, so they save time and increase efficiency by automating that selection process.

In difficult economic times, negotiating with vendors is crucial. Beth Ashmore and Jill E. Grogg offer advice to libraries on how to effectively negotiate for content, tools, and services in their article, "The Art of the Deal: Negotiation Advice from Library Leaders and Vendors" (2009). They suggest that libraries appoint more seasoned librarians to carry out the negotiations, rather than new librarians who are not as familiar with vendors, library service, and/or negotiating. Negotiation is often viewed as a responsibility that comes with collection management. Library administrators trust each collection manager to the task of negotiating contracts, regardless of their experience level. Ashmore and Grogg say, "Institutions should appoint librarians with the necessary negotiation skills needed to get better contracts, better prices, and improved vendor relationships" (2009, p.20).

This article also advises negotiators to do their research. They need to understand the vendor's products, know who their customers are, how long they have been in the industry, and who their competition is (Ashmore and Grogg, 2009, p.20). Find out what support and training there is for the product, both from the vendor itself and outside opportunities. For example, perhaps a library consortium offers training and support on a product to its constituents. Also, research what direction the vendor is headed in the future. Have they committed to keeping up with information trends and technology upgrades? The negotiator should also research the library's specific needs. Are there policy limitations, specific procedures, or mission objectives that the library needs the vendor to address? Negotiators should draw up a list of deal breakers; that is, "a simple list of must-haves and can-do-withouts" so that it is clear to the vendor and the negotiator what exactly they are looking for (Ashmore and Grogg, 2009, p.21).

Negotiating specifics of contracts and services with vendors saves money. It ensures that the library gets what they need. They are, after all, the paying customer. The quality of the library's collections may depend on the specifics of a contract. See Appendix B for more on negotiating with vendors.

Another easy way to make the most of a materials budget is to find a group to join for group discounts. Library consortia can sometimes negotiate deals for their members that benefit the whole group. State and national library associations are another group that may be able to negotiate for their members.

Alternative funding sources

Many library types can benefit from grant writing. There are a variety of grant types and granting institutions to be considered. Some require very specific projects and reporting, while others are very simple, flexible, one-time gifts. In general, grants can help pad declining materials budgets. Lois Stickell and Lisa Nickel, authors of "Grant Proposals for the Working Librarian: From Idea to Implementation" offer good advice about grant writing. They suggest that library staff start small by looking locally for smaller grants in order to get the idea of what writing, implementing, and facilitating a grant is like before going after larger sums (2011, p.49). They also point out that you can ask for copies of successful grant applications from the grant agency so that you can see what goes into a successful application (p.49).

Fundraising is another avenue to supplement library budgets. The authors of the article "Sources of Funding for Public Libraries" say, "Most libraries tend to supplement their budgets with book sales and small gifts from individuals, and while these sources are important, a more ambitious fundraising campaign should be undertaken" (Duncan et al., 1998, p.167). The authors suggest twelve steps to a successful fundraising campaign, including clearly stating the need for the funds. For example, a bookmobile's being old is not a good reason for a library to seek funds to replace it. The real reason is that a sufficient and reliable bookmobile helps the library fulfill its mission to reach out to underserved populations. This fundraising approach goes beyond used book sales, bake sales, and car washes (but may include all of those strategies). Rather, the authors suggest that libraries focus on bigger ideas, like "make arrangements for all donations to go into a fund that is tax-deductible" and "research the giving patterns of local corporations" (p.169).

Many libraries have Friends of the Library groups. These groups support the library through financial contributions and volunteer projects. Many Friends activities can supplement a library's materials budget. Friends groups often manage used book sales and solicit donations of library materials. When donations come in, library staff and Friends volunteers can go through them for titles the library can use in its collections. Out of print titles, rare editions, and extra copies of popular books and other materials can often be found within library donations. It is well worth the time and effort to enhance a library collection to go through the public's generous donations in pursuit of useful items! (See Figure 8.1.)

Often, especially in public libraries, patrons show interest in donating to the library and actually ask how they can help. There is a graceful way of accepting donations and getting what the library truly needs. Any donation is generous, but wouldn't it be nice to count on a couple of defined donations for things the library knows it needs? Consider programs like "Adopt-A-Magazine" and

Figure 8.1 Donations at a public library

"Adopt-An-Author." Patrons commit to sponsoring a magazine subscription or a certain number of copies of a popular author's next book. These programs help the library save money, and also allow selectors to rely on donors for specific items. Knowing they can spend less money on lots of copies of current bestsellers lets them commit funds to other things. Patrons are happy because they have quicker access to popular items. Hold lists may be shorter if a donor can be relied on to supplement the budget with defined items. The Friends of the Library could participate in these types of programs too. Perhaps they can commit each year to covering the expenses of a particular standing order or purchasing a more expensive reference item (like a set of encyclopedias).

Book sales were mentioned briefly above, but deserve their own discussion. An article by Cecilia Hogan titled "Library Book Sales: Cleaning House or Cleaning Up?" extols these sales as an especially good way to please both library users and library staff. There are a lot of book lovers out there who will load up on fifty-cent castoffs. Many people enjoy the nostalgia of old books or collect them. Library staff love the opportunity to unload extra copies they no longer need, outdated items they have weeded from the collection, or slightly damaged items that they have replaced with new copies. It's a win-win situation! At fifty cents or a dollar per book, Hogan says, "small libraries might make a few thousand dollars from a successful book sale" (2008, p.37).

Hogan takes the book sale idea even further. She mentions that the first people through the library doors on sale day are usually book resellers (2008, p.37). They have hand-held devices and are scanning UPC codes and typing titles into Wi-Fi enabled mobile devices. They know how to find the real gems hidden in the piles of dusty used books. They are paying fifty cents for books that may look a little worse for wear, but which they happen to know are worth far more.

This is an area where libraries may be missing out on funding opportunities. If the library has rare books, collectibles, and valuable merchandise, they should be the ones to cash in! Hogan's article lists some online tools that library book-sale organizers can use to find out the real value of the books they are selling. (See Figures 8.2 and 8.3.)

The final alternate funding source we will mention here is endowment funds. Endowments are investment funds established to support an institution like a library. When someone donates to an endowment fund, the money is invested – sometimes for something specific like library materials, and sometimes to support the work of the library more generally. Usually, these donations are tax deductible for the donors. Libraries must follow the withdrawal, usage,

Figure 8.2 Public library used book sale

Figure 8.3 Price scanner

and investment policies set for their endowment, but could certainly specify ways the money could be put toward enhancing library collections.

Formats

The variety of formats collected by all library types can either help or hurt a library's budget. Each library will have to decide if their objective is to duplicate titles in various formats (which may hurt their collection budget) or if they will focus on widening the title choices by only purchasing titles in one format (which may help the collection budget). There are library databases to supplement magazine and journal collections. There are e-book and audio book collections to supplement print collections. There are music download collections to supplement music CD collections.

Knowing what is available in a variety of formats can help selectors work together to get the most out of a collection budget. Online collections of public domain titles, such as Project Gutenberg and *bartleby.com* add another option to buying more copies in classic literature and some reference materials.

Sharing

Libraries can also make the most of their collection budgets by cooperating in sharing programs, such as interlibrary loan. Often, library branches send materials back and forth to fulfill one another's lending needs. Each branch can focus their collections in a specific way so that as a group their collections are broad. This way, no one library has to have everything for everyone. Interlibrary loan programs help every library succeed in filling their patrons' requests without taxing their budgets with purchases of unique, less popular, and sometimes obscure items.

One example of a successful sharing program is described in David Kohl and Tom Sanville's article, "More Bang for the Buck: Increasing the Effectiveness of Library Expenditures Through Cooperation" (2006). The authors suggest that there are four areas of library service in which creative use "can improve the cost–benefit ratio of library expenditures: sharing printed books, storing print materials, providing access to the journal literature electronically, and providing access to electronic versions of library special collections, faculty publications, or university projects through a consortial institutional repository" (p.395). Each library in the consortium (in this case, OhioLINK) saves money by having increased access to materials. The increase in access to information is a benefit in itself, but getting the most value out of each dollar spent was the main goal achieved. The four areas listed above are all great ways to save money, but approaching them from the consortia level lets each member library reap complete benefits without having to invest in the full amount of resources needed.

Collection philosophy

Libraries can define their collection philosophy in their collection management policy. Some libraries work toward a broad collection that covers a wide variety of subjects, but make fewer titles available in any one area. Other libraries focus on a deep collection that covers fewer topics, but provides a more profound assortment of titles on each. A library with a broad collection may be more likely to try out new formats. For example, they might provide audio books on tape, CD, MP3 players, and an e-audio collection. There are a smaller number of titles to choose from in each format, but each format is represented in the collection. A deep collection philosophy is likely to focus on one or two formats and provide more titles in each.

Each philosophy has cost implications. Rolling out new collections and formats has an associated price. Libraries need time to market and develop new collections, so they should not invest in them unless they can commit. Introducing a new collection or a new format, and then not having the money to develop it, just teases library users. Patrons will try out the new items and (hopefully) come back for more. If only a few items are available with no plan to add more, the collection can't satisfy its users. Collection budgets need to be adjusted for new collections so that they can be properly funded. New collections and formats have processing costs too. New stickers, cases, and other finding and shelving aids have to be stocked. Especially in a weak economy, a more sober approach to collection management should be taken. Don't introduce new collections, formats, shelving arrangements, displays, stickers, etc. when money is tight. They won't get the monetary attention necessary to reach their benchmark as a successful collection.

Try to see the bigger picture, and remember that everything is connected. Consider the impact of the little things in how collections are presented. One seemingly small change can impact any other part of the collection lifecycle. Consider the example of a public library patron who suggested that the library create a separate collection of "Inspirational Fiction." In order to do this, the library would need to spend time identifying all the titles in the existing fiction collection that fell under this subject. They would need to re-label, re-link, and possibly re-catalog each of these titles with the new subject information. They would need to find or create a shelving area to display them, as well as new signage. They would need to write a collection management policy for this new collection, as well as a collection objective and a benchmark. They would need to set aside funds to support this new, separate collection so that it would continue to grow and update. They would need to train staff about the new collection and assign someone to manage it. The patron just thought that moving some books to a new area would create this new collection, and it is not necessarily a bad suggestion – but it is one that the library has to plan for carefully. Making the most of a collection budget means creating collections and subdivisions within them that the library can support financially.

This philosophy discussion applies to weeding too. Choosing to have a lot of old, irrelevant items on the shelf versus having a few fresh, up-to-date items is a decision every library needs to make. Aside from archives and museums, most libraries will benefit from current collections, even if that means having fewer titles available. In fact, that extra, empty shelf space indicates to donors that more items are needed. When the shelves are packed with old items, people may think the library has plenty, when in fact they are in need.

The final piece of this budget discussion goes back to library staff communications with their users. Staff need to be careful to not call library services and collections "free." The vast majority of libraries are funded somehow, and very often through the tax dollars of their users. Staff should point out to their users whenever possible that the library exists because users are the ones that directly fund it. Being able to recite the costs of services and collections is a great way to show stakeholders that staff are mindful, careful, and attentive to how the library budget is spent.

Everything is connected

Abstract: A successful and quality-driven library should be holistic in nature. This chapter outlines the interconnectedness of four library resources: staff, collection, facility, and technology. A quality collection is achieved when library staff around the building and throughout its departments understand the collection's purpose as it fits into the bigger picture of the library mission.

Key words: holistic, staff, technology, community center, collaboration, job shadowing, peer review, core competencies, holistic budgeting, holistic evaluation.

Throughout this book we have stressed what we call "holistic library service." This truly means that everything is connected. The purpose of this chapter is to analyze how holistic library service is created and delivered. We will also discuss how a quality collection relies on a holistic approach.

Using the four critical resources for library service emphasized by Sandra Nelson, author of *Implementing for Results: Your Strategic Plan in Action*, we can illustrate how various areas of library service are related. The four resources Nelson emphasizes are staff, collection, facility, and technology (2009, p. 134). Each resource contributes to a quality collection, and also to the quality of service in each of the other areas.

Holistic library service

Holistic libraries credit each department and service as contributors to their overall success. Each department and service enhances the others, creating a library that fully impacts its users. Holistic library service is more than cross-promotion of the multiple functions the library serves to its various users. It includes a vision of a library system that enriches lives, and is executed by each staff person at every level of library service. Holistic library service is created by a library whose staff understands and contributes to the bigger picture. Patrons believe in the library's mission and its relevance to their lives. They turn to the library first, counting on it to satisfy their information, research, entertainment, and cultural needs. Holistic libraries recognize those individual needs and translate them into services for their whole communities. They become community centers.

The 2008 Gale/*Library Journal* Library of the Year is an excellent example of a library that embraces holistic service (Berry, 2008). The Laramie County Library System (LCLS) in Cheyenne, Wyoming was completed in 2007. One of their patrons called it "a place so extraordinary in its function and design, that it has become the spontaneous center of our community" (Berry, 2008, p. 35). *Library Journal* says, "The impact of LCLS is the anticipated result of a carefully planned and brilliantly executed vision and mission that grew out of the library's relationship with the people it serves" (p. 34) and continues with "The LCLS staff are alert to the imperative to meet both individual needs and those of the community as a whole" (p. 35). County Librarian, Lucie Osborn, said, "Public libraries have an even stronger role to play in our society than they have in the past. They must be the community center, the destination" (Berry, 2008, p. 37). That, in a nutshell, is the result of holistic library service.

How staff impact collections in a holistic library

Libraries have very diverse staffs in terms of knowledge, skill set, and talent within an individual organization. Any one academic library, for example, could have reference staff, catalogers, collection development specialists, archivists, circulation staff, shelvers, building maintenance, grant writers and fund raisers, information technology specialists, and technical services staff. Public libraries could add children's librarians, teen librarians, outreach librarians, public relations specialists, and a whole host of paraprofessionals in every department as well. It is a challenge for people in these differing departments, who perform different kinds of work and carry out different daily tasks, to work holistically. In actuality, each person does contribute to the library's mission. It is important that they understand how their work impacts other areas so that their priorities mesh with those of their colleagues and those of the library as a whole. We have seen evidence of this relationship throughout this book. Staff at each phase of the collection life cycle perform tasks and make decisions that impact the quality of the overall collection. Let's reiterate with some examples.

Selectors make purchasing decisions for the collection that determine its strengths and weaknesses in different subject areas. We mentioned the philosophy of a broad collection vs. a deep collection. The makeup of the library collection is determined by those who select the materials. Selection has perhaps the biggest impact on collection quality because the success or failure of a library to satisfy its users depends on the materials it makes available.

Collection maintainers make weeding decisions for the collection that impact on its relevance to library users, its currency, and its physical condition. Weeding also affects shelving staff because it creates shelf space. Shelvers will need to balance the shelves by shifting other materials into the new spaces created by de-selection. The reverse, when weeding is neglected, affects shelvers because they struggle to find space for items added to the collection.

Technical services staff decide what kind of processing an item will receive, which affects a collection's physical attractiveness and usefulness to users. It also affects consistency of labeling throughout a collection and library users' ability to locate specific items. Technical services staff are directly affected by selection choices because they are the ones who catalog and process the items added to the collection.

Many different staffers identify and repair broken items. Shelvers may find these items in the stacks, and circulation staff may see them at check-in and check-out. Technical services staff may even identify defective items that are new to the collection, received that way from the manufacturer or printer. We've said several times that a quality collection is one that works, and many staffers have the ability to identify damaged items throughout the collection life cycle.

Catalogers ensure findability of items in the library's online catalog. The records they choose to bring into their catalog when copy cataloging must accurately describe the items the library owns. Catalogers choose what records are linked to which library materials. They affect library users' as well as reference staff's ability to locate titles in the collection. When original cataloging is performed, catalogers are trusted to accurately describe library materials. They choose the subject headings, enter the publication information, and define the item type (format) and shelf location (collection) when linking. All of this information is used at various stages of the life cycle.

When reference staff are aware of collections and titles, the whole collection becomes more accessible to patrons. When library users ask for reference or reader's advisory assistance, they expect the staff to understand and be familiar with the collection. Bibliographic instruction comes into play when patrons ask for specific help in using library resources. In this case, staff directly impact the usefulness of the collection because they teach people how to use and evaluate the information contained in library materials. This applies to all formats in which the library delivers information.

Circulation staff check materials in and out to patrons. An item's status at any given time is dependent on this. When circulation staff make a mistake, perhaps missing one item in a pile at check-out, the quality of the collection and the work of other staff members are affected. Reference librarians have to believe that when they look up an item in the catalog, a status of "available" or "checked-in" means that the item is on the shelf, ready for use. When this is not the case, they fail to fulfill their patron's need. Circulation is the flow of materials through the system, so it is a crucial point that affects collection quality.

Shelvers ensure findability of items returned to shelves. Their work is the go-between from circulation to reference. When circulation checks an item back in, shelvers put it back on the shelf for re-use. Now reference librarians can help library users find those materials to re-start the cycle.

These are just a few examples, but it is clear that staff members in every department make decisions and perform work that affect collections at every point in their life cycle. Communication between staff in every department is crucial. When they understand the work of their counterparts in other departments, they can track and fix – and prevent – problems more easily.

There are measures that managers can take to create a more holistic staff. One idea is cross-training. The more aware staff are to the challenges and contributions of their co-workers, the more they will understand the bigger picture of library service. They will also be able to help each other out, filling in as necessary in other capacities. It is dangerous to have only one employee who knows the ins and outs of a project or duty. There is no one to perform quality checks on that person. As uncomfortable as it makes us, a "fiery crash" scenario is important too. It would be unfortunate to have all known information and experience in any work area leave (or even die) with someone. We have discussed the idea that a quality collection requires smooth transitions between workflows and parts of the collection life cycle. If only one staff person knows how to perform a particular action somewhere inside the workflow or life cycle, the collection suffers. A bottleneck is formed until someone else can step in. A holistic staff is one that is aware of the bigger picture, and has enough cross-trained staff that backup is readily available at all phases of the life cycle. This benefits individual employees, too, broadening the scope of their skills. An article by Kristy Leung written for *South China Morning Post* gives a wonderful international example of this (2009). She speaks of the hospitality industry, but it clearly applies to libraries. She says, "In the hospitality industry, operations must be smooth at all times. To accomplish this, staff in each department should understand what their colleagues elsewhere are doing and why. This makes for closer co-operation, enhanced team spirit and better customer service". She goes on to explain that "Apart from that, the training also allows us to see the potential of staff ... And, of course, [individuals] have an opportunity to explore their own talent" (Leung, 2009). Holistic libraries with quality collections embody this idea of close co-operation, team spirit, and customer service.

Job shadowing is one way to help staff understand each other's actions and contributions. For example, someone from purchasing can spend an afternoon with someone whose job is processing. Or, information technology staff can observe while selectors make their final decisions. When individuals have experienced the work of other departments, they begin to see how each part makes up the whole, and how each part is important to the whole. This, in turn, creates staff buy-in to the library's vision and mission. This idea is confirmed in Kathleen Corlett's article, "Best Job Shadowing" (2009, p.7). She gives the example of a chemical distribution company that has a job shadowing component to their training program for new employees. Each new employee spends time in various departments, such as customer service, sales support, and accounting. The hope is that they will understand their new job responsibilities better if they know how their role fits in with the others. Libraries could certainly benefit from this approach. If each new employee observed the work performed in different departments, even for a short time, each department would have greater respect for each other and their roles.

Peer reviews are another way to foster a holistic staff. In this case, it is those who work most closely together that learn more about each other. When it is time for managers to do annual performance reviews, they can ask a few of each employee's closest co-workers (in terms of overlapping work, not close friendships, although those characteristics may overlap) to answer some questions about each other. They can list a few ways that the employee best contributes to the department or project and a few areas that the employee could focus on improving. These reviews can be anonymous or not, depending on individual situations and circumstances.

A holistic staff has a stake in helping their co-workers succeed. This is a nice opportunity for those who work most closely together to recognize each other's work. Knowing your desk-mate will be weighing in on your performance review could encourage you to communicate and collaborate better!

How staff impact the facility

Library facilities house the collections that are maintained by library staff. That is the connection between staff, facilities, and collections. How do the decisions made by staff at every phase of library service affect the facilities that house library collections?

Reference staff may be involved in deciding where to house each collection. Does a map collection belong on shelves with large, pull-out drawers? Do children's materials belong on lower shelves within reach of small children? Should materials for low-vision patrons, such as large print and audio books, be placed on the library's street level so that those with mobility challenges can more easily access them? Reference staff are directly related to a collection's use, so they are the appropriate staff to weigh in on how and where collections are shelved.

Technical services staff determine the kind of packaging in which various items will be processed. If they choose a bag that needs to hang, the library facility must have a place for a rack to hang them on. If they choose a very large case to hold an item with lots of parts, wide or tall shelving must accommodate that choice.

Pages may need special carts or shelving areas to hold items waiting to be returned to the shelf. They may also require space to sort these items.

Maintenance staff keep facilities in good working order so that library users can comfortably and safely use library collections. They may repair shelves, help move shelving units to more useful or efficient areas, or even build new shelving solutions for special materials.

Archivists are very involved in the facilities that house special collections. Fragile documents may need air-tight or light-proof storage spaces that are temperature controlled.

Libraries today have spaces for more types of activities than ever. In a public library, there are services and collections to be viewed (movies), listened to (audio books or music), read aloud (story time, "big books"), played with (puzzles, game consoles, puppets), computed (CD-ROMs, Internet, computer instruction classes), or read silently (newspapers, magazines, books) . . . and probably others too! Maker spaces and digital labs are becoming more and more popular, and they require special facilities as well (sound proofing, space for large equipment like 3-D printers, wiring for lots of electronics, etc.)

Facilities, collections, and staff are all connected in this idea: staff manage the collections and facilities, facilities house the collections and the places to enjoy the collections, and a quality collection is one that is used. Holistic library service not only provides the collections, but has a facility with places to enjoy them. Sure, library users can check materials out and enjoy them at home, but libraries could have viewing and listening stations, places to read aloud and play with children, and places for quiet enjoyment of library collections too. That fosters the community-center idea; that residents come to the library just to be there and enjoy each other and the space, not only to find items to take back home.

How staff impact technology

Many libraries of various types have electronic collections. They have electronic serials, pages of reference web links, e-book collections, blogs, wikis, training tutorials, and more. Staff impact the use of technology-based collections in holistic libraries in ways such as these:

Reference staff train patrons in the use and accessibility of electronic collections of all kinds. They may hold classes for many people at once or offer one-on-one sessions. Holistic libraries do not make a distinction between traditional reference questions where, perhaps, patrons ask for research help or help finding the answer to a specific question, and a technical support question. Libraries that are community centers, and relevant to the needs of their users, understand that it is not the responsibility of library users to know what they can ask of whom. They need help; they assume library staff are there to help them. Those who provide reference service in modern libraries need to have core technology competencies so that they can provide core technical support to their patrons. The fact is, library users in all kinds of libraries need help using technology, and holistic libraries offer both electronic resources and expertise to support them. It is noted that reference staff probably do not have advanced degrees in technology, but they do need core competencies to help their users. One source for core competency definitions and training is Web Junction (*webjunction.org*).

IT staff make available the hardware, software, and infrastructure that electronic collections require. There is a delicate balance between reference staff, who are charged with helping library users find and evaluate information in a variety of formats, and IT staff, who are charged with keeping the library's networks secure, balancing the bandwidth load so that each electronic service the library supports is reliable and available, and keeping the library's resources up-to-date. Reference staff want to give access and IT staff sometimes need to restrict that access for the safety and security of the network. After all, libraries have sensitive patron information on their servers. They keep track of patron contact information like address and phone number, as well as what titles are checked out by each user. This information has to be saved long enough for the library to track its holdings. It is imperative that they uphold patron privacy, but equally important that they have access to certain private information on their network servers for a certain amount of time. These are two departments that must come to an understanding in order to become holistic. They have to understand the struggles of the other and find a way to provide excellent customer service and just the right balance of access and restriction.

Catalogers create records that link users to specific titles in electronic collections. Many libraries have e-book collections, and they want their users to find those titles in the online catalog. Third party collections like these need to be brought into the ILS to allow them to be searched. Some of the newer patron catalog systems allow web resources to be searched in addition to the library's physical holdings. A staff person has to interact with the technology in order to create this catalog link. In fact, some of the newest integrated library systems even have catalog overlays that allow patrons to download e-books and other digital content from third party vendors right in the catalog itself, without the need to be linked to the third party platform at all. Holistic library collections make all relevant, authoritative, and current information available to their users, and these links facilitate that success.

Staff need to be aware of and trained to troubleshoot more and more technology services all the time. Mobile apps, SMS services, self-service fee payment, and even augmented reality programs are making library collections and services more accessible than ever. The staff has to learn to create that content, market it, teach it, and even use it themselves.

All staff members require training when electronic collections are enhanced, upgraded, or newly acquired. Untrained staff can negatively impact the accessibility, promotion, and use of these collections. Web designers and other electronic services staff impact the currency and relevancy of information in their electronic collections. Broken web links, files in obsolete formats, or blogs and wikis with no current entries are useless to library users.

Connections to other library services

It is clear that staff decisions impact a quality collection in terms of the collections themselves, the facilities that house them, and the technology they embody. To continue with how collections impact facilities and technology and how facilities impact technology would be redundant. Those connections are implicit in the lists above. Understand that in holistic libraries, each of the four categories is interconnected, and each contributes to a library's mission, goals, and how it translates them to services for library users.

There are a few other areas of library service that also have connections in holistic environments. One is programming. Library programming includes events such as lectures by faculty members about their new research at a university library, a hands-on painting class at a public library, or a storyteller at a school library. These are just a few examples, but library programming is an important contributor to library missions of providing cultural experiences, lifelong learning opportunities, or the support of entertainment and research needs. Programming in a holistic library is connected to collections, staff, facilities, and technology. Staff plan programs that are of interest in their communities. They may plan programs on a topic that is recurring at the reference desk. For example, when new tax laws are passed that benefit first time homebuyers, a public library may get a lot of questions about it at their reference desk. They may decide to find a speaker in the law or real estate industry who can inform an audience all about the first-time homebuyer law. It is a strategy for relaying current interest, authoritative, and relevant information to many people in the community all at once. The facility is connected because the library must provide a space to hold the program. In addition to needing space to hold the program, they also need space to display information advertising the program and space to hold new library materials on the subject of the program. Technology required for the program could be presentation software, a projector, an Internet connection so that the speaker can share information on the web with attendees, and even a microphone for the speaker. Some libraries even webcast their programs, or record them to link their web pages to the program video for "virtual attendance." Holistic libraries need each of these pieces to fall into place in order to present successful programs.

Another connection holistic libraries make is in budgeting. Our previous chapter discussed how to make the most of a collection budget in a line item budget. Here, we can take a wider view of the library's entire budget. An article by D'Llle Asantewa called "Holistic Budgeting: A Process: A Whole System Approach" discusses holistic practices from a budgeting perspective (2003). The author describes how program budgeting is more holistic than line item budgeting. Program budgeting looks at organizational goals, needs, and capabilities. It "aligns library objectives with the financial ability to support them" (Asantewa, 2003, p. 18). It also "reflects the whole system's efforts to express perceptions of how to make the most of organizational strengths and opportunities, how to strengthen organizational weaknesses, and how to ward off threats to the library community" (p. 18). In other words, money is put into programs that advance the library's goals. (To clarify, here we are not talking necessarily about programs as "events," but more as general activities and projects.) Line-item budgets focus on expenditures like salaries, equipment, and supplies. One would hope that putting money into salaries and benefits translates to a well-trained, well-compensated staff that is loyal and satisfied. However, funding a staffing "program" that has specific goals of increasing staff training, raising job satisfaction, and improving the physical health and well-being of staff through retirement and insurance benefits packages is a more holistic way to budget. It takes into account the goals of training, compensation, and satisfaction, which are only *hoped for*, but not worked toward with focus in a line-item budget.

Let's look at the equipment example. Libraries may want to purchase equipment like document scanners so that they can preserve their local newspaper archives through digitization. In a line item budget, they simply put money into the equipment line and purchase the scanners. However, they also need to build money into other lines of the budget in order to reach their goal. They need more technical services staff to catalog and index the digitized files and more IT staff to create a searchable platform for the finished product. They need to build time and training – maybe even a trainer – into the budget to bring staff up to speed on how to use the final product. Most libraries, especially in these economic times, do not have extra money to add to various lines of a budget. They end up sacrificing a good project like digitization because they can't complete it properly, or piecing it together over a few years' time.

In a program budget, the library sets a goal and then decides on all of the funding the project will require. Since there is no equipment line, staffing line, or salaries line, they simply put the necessary money into the project. If the digitization project requires the resources listed above, the budget reflects that. Of course, library budgets are not unlimited. In order to add tech services and IT time to the digitization project, perhaps another program led by that department will have to be limited. For example, let's say that a library's web page was overhauled one year with the goal of making it more user-friendly. That year, time and resources were put into that project. The next year, when the web page is complete and the goal has been met, less time can be spent on it and more time on a new project. This is the way many departments with line-item budgets are run too, but with the emphasis on the separate pieces of the project – the equipment, the staff, or the training that are budgeted for separately – not on the goal of the program itself. Holistic program budgets focus on the goal and fund all the necessary pieces to achieve it.

Quality collections and connecting library services now come back into focus. Holistic budgeting practices, such as program budgeting described above, create quality collections because the goals of the collection management policy are the focus. If a library were to add a new collection, it is more likely to be funded than in a line-item budget where each collection is allotted its separate piece. Libraries that assign dollar amounts yearly to serials, audio books, or databases, for example, treat those collections as separate entities. If they want to add a new collection, such as e-audio books, they have to find a line to take the money from. A library with a program budget can fund the goal to increase the relevancy of their audio book collection through the addition of a new downloadable format. Perhaps they need to purchase fewer titles in an older format that year, or redirect resources from a program completed in a previous year to this new service, but they have created a quality collection that is funded, has a collection objective, and that connects the four areas of library service (again: staff, collection, facility, and technology).

Staff buy-in to library projects is more likely with this program budget model because money is not taken from "their" budget to fund projects that are not entirely within "their" domain. In many libraries, staff manage budgets for specific areas (like technology, materials, or events). Since a program budget doesn't piece money from several areas, no one has to sacrifice money they may have had other plans for. Each member of staff contributes to the bigger program goal of the library. Staff are less territorial over "their" areas and "their" budgets, and more in tune to the programs being offered by the library. Staff may also find that their skills become more diversified in this model. They don't become pigeon-holed into one area of library service, but can contribute to a program in a variety of ways, outside of an assigned budget area.

Evaluating library services holistically

Library staff constantly evaluate the services they offer. It helps them to justify those services and ensures that they remain relevant to their users by adding new ones. Many libraries evaluate each service separately and make decisions about them individually. This is especially true when a large staff has broken down responsibilities to one piece of a collection or program. How can a library determine that they have a quality collection if each person only sees a small part?

We have emphasized in this chapter that everything is connected; that library staff in various departments need to communicate with each other to ensure cohesion. This is absolutely crucial in the evaluation phase. If, for example, a selector is responsible for purchasing for the business collection, that person needs to be aware of what selectors in related categories are choosing. Some social science topics overlap, such as careers, real estate, and personal finance. Selectors in related fields need to be aware of the resources that connect them. A quality collection is shaped by those connections. Scott Nicholson (2004) says, in his article, "A Conceptual Framework for the Holistic Measurement and Cumulative Evaluation of Library Services" that "In the context of measurement and evaluation, it means that a more thorough knowledge and understanding of a system can be gained from combining different measures than can be derived than taking those measures separately."

Nicholson also says, "the complexity of users, systems, and processes is all connected; problems in one area may come from another area of the system." What if a library, through holistic evaluation of their collections, finds that they have reference librarians who are strong in a particular area (for example, librarians with advanced degrees in business), but that the library's business collection is weak? Their collection goal may change based on the expertise of those who use it. On the flip side, if a library has a strong business collection but librarians who are weak in the understanding of its use, this strong collection still becomes a weak part of the library's services. Holistic evaluation takes into account not only the collection itself, but the people who serve it. The connection between staff and collection has affected the library's ability to serve its users in this scenario.

Conclusion

Holistic library service unites departments, programs, and people. It results in strong systems that support each other. Evaluating library services by considering the connections between resources like staff, collection, facility, and technology is important because it shows decision makers the bigger picture. The viewpoints from different departments are represented in decision making, and departments will have complementary missions, goals, and objectives. Library staff in all departments should find their work more satisfying when they see themselves reflected in the final product: the service that the library offers. In this case, a quality collection is achieved when people who work on each phase of the collection's life cycle respect other staff's contributions and understand the collection's purpose as a whole.

Appendix A: Public library collection management policy

Appendix Contents

Books – fiction, nonfiction, large print, reference materials

Periodicals and newspapers

Audio books and electronic books

Video/DVD recordings

Music recordings

Miscellaneous collections

English as a Second Language (ESL)/adult literacy

Local history collection

Books – picture books, easy readers, and fiction

I. Introduction – date last updated: _____

The library will acquire materials for general information and entertainment needs that will benefit the patrons of the [Public Library]. The purpose of this collection development policy is to provide guidelines for the selection of library materials, enabling staff to build and maintain a collection which reflects the mission and goals of the library and which meets the needs of the community. The policy explains the criteria for the selection, evaluation, and de-selection of all library materials, and can be used to help answer questions from the public regarding the inclusion or absence of certain materials in the collection.

This collection management policy is a statement and guide to be used by the [Public Library] in selection, acquisition, evaluation, de-selection (weeding), preservation and maintenance of the library collection. It is understood that as the community changes, the collection management policy will change as well. In order to keep the policy current and relevant, sections might be changed and amended as needed. These changes will be marked with appropriate dates.

II. Community profile – date last updated: _____

The [Public Library] serves the city of [City] and [Township]. This service area encompasses [County/Region].

[City] began as a farming community. While farms and horse ranches still make up much of [Township], the area is becoming more residential as new housing is built.

Employment demographics from the U.S. Census (*census. gov*) when compared with population statistics for this service area, indicate a large commuter population. Many working people in this service area commute to jobs in surrounding towns.

The 2000 census shows that this service area is made up of primarily white, middle class people. A rise in Black, Asian, and multi-racial populations is shown between the 1990 and 2000 censuses, but these groups still make up less than 4 percent of the total population of the service area. The vast majority of the population speaks English at home.

Finally, the 2000 census shows that the majority of the population of this service area is between 35 and 64 years old. SEMCOG (*semcog.org*) projects a large increase in the 65+ age group by 2030.

These figures indicate that the [City] community would best benefit from a library collection of popular interest, general information materials in a variety of formats. There is little indication of the need for materials in non-English languages, academic research resources, or other highly specific interest areas at this time.

III. Mission statement – date last updated: _____

The mission of the [Public Library] is to offer patron-centered library services with diverse materials to support the reading interests, information needs, and lifelong learning require-ments of a changing community.

IV. Selection responsibility – date last updated: _____

The authority and responsibility for the selection/de-selection of library materials is delegated by the Board of Trustees to the Library Director, and under his/her direction, to the professional staff working within the various areas of service. All staff members and the general public are welcome to recommend materials for inclusion in the collection; however, the final decision rests with the Library Director.

Patrons who wish to make a suggestion for additions to the collection should speak to any of the librarians directly. There are also suggestion boxes located throughout the library. If the suggested item meets the criteria designated within the collection development policy, and if funds are available, the item may be considered for purchase.

V. General selection criteria – date last updated: _____

Since the mission of the [Public Library] is one of general entertainment and information needs, the collection of the library will be that of a popular materials library. The library will also collect items appropriate for a variety of ages. Selection of library materials will be as objective as possible. Constraints considered by the librarians will be space availability, durability, ease of format, and budget.

When making selection decisions, the librarians will rely upon a number of tools. Librarians may use reviews of materials published in professional journals as well as general interest periodicals, bibliographic listings, catalogs, and publication announcements. Materials that are deemed appropriate to the collection, but not necessarily appropriate for children and teens will be shelved in the adult collection at the discretion of the librarians.

Selection of a work does not necessarily imply the library's approval of the actions or ideas contained in that work. Materials are evaluated as a whole and not on the basis of a particular passage or passages. A work will not be automatically excluded from the library's collection because of frankness of expression or differing beliefs. In general, the [Public Library] aspires to build a broad collection based on community needs and wants. Further, the [Public Library] will aspire to build a collection that is unique and culturally significant to its community residents.

VI. Adult collection – date last updated: _____

Books – fiction, nonfiction, large print, reference materials

In addition to the general criteria, the library will include in its collection, materials based on:

- Current and anticipated patron demand.
- Popularity of the author and/or publisher.
- Attention given by critics, reviewers, professional book selection aids and the public.
- Inclusion in lists such as the *New York Times* bestseller list, the Pulitzer and Booker prize winners, the National Book Award winners, and other book lists generated by recognized authorities.
- Cultural or historical significance.

- Accurate and authoritative information.
- Relationship to existing materials in the collection on the same subject (except to complete a popular series, or to fill information gaps in the collection).
- Cost as related to estimated patron use.
- Local, state or regional significance.
- Durability and stability of binding or packaging.

Periodicals and newspapers

The library will subscribe to periodicals that cover a range of subjects of reference value and recreational interest. Preference will be given to general readership periodicals rather than professional journals due to the availability of indexed databases. The library will also subscribe to a selection of local and national newspapers.

Audio books and electronic books

The primary purpose for purchasing audio books is to provide public access to spoken recordings of print material. This will include, but not be limited to, unabridged works of fiction, nonfiction, poetry, drama, foreign language instruction, and self-improvement or instructional material. Criteria to be considered include:

- Physical quality of format.
- Reputation of the vendor and replacement policies.
- Performance quality.
- Popularly accepted formats.
- Cost related to estimated patron use.

Video/DVD recordings

Video recordings are purchased for the primary purpose of home entertainment, information, and instruction. Emphasis will be placed on video recordings that demonstrate:

- Popular demand.
- Educational and instructional value.
- Dramatizations of works of classic and popular literature.
- Dramatizations of historical events.
- Acclaimed/recognized or award-winning titles.
- Cost related to estimated patron use.

Music recordings

The library will purchase music recordings in a variety of genres. Emphasis will be placed on music recordings that meet the following criteria:

- Acclaimed/recognized or award-winning songs and musicians.
- Soundtracks of award-winning movies.
- Music recordings of historical or traditional social significance.
- Cost related to estimated patron use.

Miscellaneous collections

The library will also maintain several miscellaneous collections addressing the specific interests and needs of the community.

English as a Second Language (ESL)/adult literacy

The library will maintain a limited collection of materials based on community demand and need of ESL and adult literacy. These materials will include but are not limited to books, video, audio, and electronic data.

Local history collection

The library maintains a limited collection of local historical information. Working in conjunction with local historians and historical societies, the library will collect, preserve, organize, and make available suitable materials of historical, geographical, cultural, and genealogical relevance to the [City] area and to [State] in general. The purpose of this collection is to provide materials for historical research to visitors, newcomers, students, and other interested members of the community. In addition, the library will maintain a digitized CD-ROM collection of the [local newspaper], which includes issues back to 1929.

This collection is made up largely of gifts, and the library will only buy material for this collection where availability, space, and budgetary considerations allow. [Public Library] does not have facilities to provide museum standard or archival quality storage for materials.

VII. Juvenile collection – date last updated: _____

Materials purchased for the youth collection are subject to the same criteria as those outlined for the adult collection.

Librarians who purchase in this area use their own expertise, professional journals, patron requests, and noteworthy awards in the area of children's literature to aid in their selection. The librarians will rely on selection tools and professional journals as well as other bibliographic materials available.

The Juvenile collection has been developed to meet the entertainment, cultural, and informational needs of the [Public Library's] young patrons: infants through fifth grade. The library does not stand in loco parentis, and leaves the responsibility of guiding a minor's selections to the parent. Purchases for the collection are made to provide a wide variety of materials to meet these needs and to appeal to the wide range of interests and reading abilities common to this age group.

Books – picture books, easy readers, and fiction

In addition to the general criteria, the library will include in its picture book, easy readers, and fiction collections current, popular materials based on:

- Current and anticipated patron demand.
- Popularity of the author.
- Attention given by critics, reviewers, professional book selection aids, and the public.
- Award winners.
- Cost as related to estimated patron use.
- Local, state or regional significance.
- Durability or stability of binding or packaging.

Books – nonfiction and reference

The library will collect nonfiction in a variety of areas. Selection of materials will be based on the criteria stated above, plus:

- Accurate and authoritative information.
- Reputation of the publisher or producer.
- Relationship to existing materials in the collection on the same subject (except to complete a series, or to fill information gaps in the collection).
- Cost as related to estimated patron use.
- Present and potential relevance to community needs.
- Importance and social significance.
- Local, state or regional significance.
- Durability and stability of binding or packaging.

Periodicals

The library will subscribe to periodicals that cover a wide range of subjects of educational value and recreational interest to children.

Audio books and media kits

The primary purpose for purchasing audio books is to provide public access to spoken recordings of original print material. This will include, but not be limited to works of fiction, nonfiction, and foreign language instruction. Criteria to be considered include:

- Physical quality of format.
- Ease and speed of replacement.

- Performance quality.
- Cost as related to estimated patron use.

Such recordings may be purchased as availability and patron-demand warrants.

Video/DVD recordings

Age appropriate video recordings are purchased for the primary purpose of home entertainment, information, and instruction. Emphasis will be placed on video recordings that demonstrate:

- Informational and instructional value.
- Dramatizations of works of classic and popular literature.
- Dramatizations of historical events.
- Award-winning titles.
- Popular interest among families and children.
- Cost as related to estimated patron use.

Music recordings

The library will purchase music recordings in a variety of genres to meet patron demands. Emphasis will be placed on music recordings that meet the following criteria:

- Award-winning songs and musicians.
- Soundtracks of award-winning and popular movies.
- Music recordings of historical or traditional social significance.
- Music of popular interest.
- Cost as related to estimated patron use.

Computer software

The library will purchase software, which provides a representative range of subjects for all ages, based on:

- Educational and instructional value.
- Quality of documentation that accompanies the product.
- Ease of use for general public.
- Popularity of format and system compatibility.
- Cost as related to estimated patron use.

Realia

Realia are tangible, three-dimensional physical objects of, or from, the real world. The library will purchase realia including but not limited to puzzles, posters, and puppets and other material for use in the Children's section.

VIII. Teen collection – date last updated: _____

Purchases for the teen collection are primarily made to fill a transitional need between the children's and adult collections and are therefore limited in nature. Teens may find additional materials of interest in both the juvenile and adult collection areas. The library does not stand in loco parentis, and leaves the responsibility of guiding a minor's selections to the parent. The library encourages the public to talk to any librarian about specific materials and the selection process. Materials located in the teen area are aimed at youth, aged between 11 and 18, and include the following:

Books – fiction

In addition to the general criteria, the library will include in its fiction collection current, popular materials based on:

- Current and anticipated patron demand.
- Popularity of the author.
- Attention given by critics, reviewers, professional book selection aids, and the public.
- Award winners.
- Cost as related to estimated patron use.

Books – nonfiction

The library will collect nonfiction. Selection of materials will be based on the criteria stated above, plus:

- Accurate and authoritative information.
- Reputation of the publisher or producer.
- Relationship to existing materials in the collection on the same subject (except to complete a popular series, or to fill information gaps in the collection).
- Cost as related to estimated patron use.
- Present and potential relevance to community needs.
- Importance and social significance.
- Local, state or regional significance.
- Durability and stability of binding or packaging.

Periodicals and newspapers

The library will subscribe to periodicals that cover a variety of subjects of reference value and recreational interest to teens.

Audio books and electronic books

The primary purpose for purchasing audio books is to provide public access to spoken recordings of original print material. Criteria to be considered include:

- Physical quality of format.
- Ease and speed of replacement.
- Performance quality.
- Cost as related to estimated patron use.

Such recordings may be purchased in a variety of formats, as availability, cost, and patron demand warrant.

Music recordings

The library will purchase age appropriate music recordings in a variety of genres to meet patron demands. Emphasis will be placed on music recordings that meet the following criteria:

- Award-winning songs and musicians.
- Soundtracks of award-winning movies.
- Music recordings of historical or traditional social significance.
- Cost as related to estimated patron use.
- Durability of format.

IX. Intellectual freedom – date last updated: _____

The [Public Library] is committed to providing a library collection free from censorship and suppression. The choice of library materials by users is an individual matter. Responsibility for selecting materials for children and adolescents rests with their parents and legal guardians. While a person may reject materials for him/herself and for his/her children, he/she cannot exercise censorship to restrict access to materials for others.

The library supports intellectual freedom and endorses the following intellectual freedom statements:

- Freedom to Read (American Library Association).

- Freedom to View (Educational Film Library Association).

- The Library Bill of Rights (American Library Association).

- Diversity in Collection Development.

- Free Access to Libraries for Minors.

- Expurgation of Library Materials.

- Evaluating Library Collections.

- Restricted Access to Library Materials.

- Statement on Labeling.

- Challenged Materials.

Please see Intellectual freedom statements on p. 178 for details on these.

Access to information via the Internet – date last updated: _____

The [Public Library] provides Internet access from designated computer terminals in the library. Please refer to the [Public Library's] acceptable internet use policy, [policy number], which allows the library to conform to Public Act 212 of 2000.

Challenges to materials in the collection – date last updated: _____

The American Library Association Library Bill of Rights Article I states "Materials should not be excluded because of their origin, background, or views of those contributing to their creation." Article II further states "Materials should not be proscribed or removed because of partisan or doctrinal disapproval." Librarians are receptive to comments regarding the collection and will discuss with any citizen concepts outlined in the collection policy. Citizens wishing to formalize a comment regarding an item in the collection will be referred to the librarians and the library will follow a standard procedure for handling complaints and comments regarding library materials.

X. Gifts – date last updated: _____

Please refer to [Public Library] [policy number].

XI. Cooperatives and resource sharing – date last updated: _____

Since no individual library has the resources available to meet all user needs, interlibrary loan service is provided within the cooperative and participating libraries. It supplements and greatly expands local collections, removes geographic barriers and is essential to libraries of all types and sizes. To that end, the [Public Library] participates in regional and state cooperative programs to provide a full range of access to information to its patrons.

The [Public Library] is a member of [library cooperative], which provides a comprehensive program of support services for member libraries. These services include resource sharing and professional development of staff.

XII. Preservation and conservation – date last updated: _____

The library will make all attempts possible to maintain a healthful environment for housing the collection. In the event of a disaster, such as flooding, fire, smoke damage, etc., conservation and preservation will be attempted.

The library will make all attempts possible to repair damaged library materials. Items that are damaged beyond in-house repair attempts may be considered for replacement if they meet current collection management criteria as outlined in this policy.

Items that are damaged beyond repair will be recycled whenever possible.

XIII. De-selection (weeding) – date last updated: _____

The [Public Library] is committed to providing a dynamic, useful, and up to date collection for the general public. In order to provide this, the library will undertake de-selection (weeding) when appropriate. The librarians will generally de-select library materials under the following circumstances.

- Materials in poor condition.
- Obsolete or inaccurate information.

- Obsolete formats.
- Space considerations.
- Unnecessary duplication.
- Poorly or under-circulated materials.

These criteria are by no means a comprehensive list. Librarians will make the final judgment of materials to be withdrawn. De-selected materials will become part of the Friends of the Library Book Sale or recycled where appropriate.

XIV. Evaluation and revisions – date last updated: _____

The library is aware that we are living in a period of great technological change, especially in regards to the information industry. In order to maintain a collection that continues to serve the patrons of the [Public Library] well into the future, it will be necessary to review portions of this policy periodically. The librarians will make recommendations for revisions to the policy based upon surveys, circulation statistics, expressed public opinions, and current market trends.

XV. Conclusion – date last updated: _____

The [Public Library] has created this collection development policy to inform the public on the scope and nature of the collection. The goal of the staff of the [Public Library] is to create a useful, relevant collection that serves the population of the library district. Comments and questions regarding the policy may be directed toward any librarian.

Intellectual freedom statements

Statements on intellectual freedom from the American Library Association:

Freedom to Read

Freedom to View

Library Bill of Rights

Diversity in Collection Development (An Interpretation of the Library Bill of Rights)

Free Access to Libraries for Minors (An Interpretation of the Library Bill of Rights)

Expurgation of Library Materials (An Interpretation of the Library Bill of Rights)

Evaluating Library Collections (An Interpretation of the Library Bill of Rights)

Restricted Access to Library Materials (An Interpretation of the Library Bill of Rights)

Statement on Labeling

Challenged Materials (An Interpretation of the Library Bill of Rights)

All statements are available online from *ala.org*

Appendix B: Strategic content negotiation for the small library

Sophia Guevara, Research Librarian, W.K. Kellogg Foundation

Introduction

With shrinking budgets, today's information professionals are pressed to make tough decisions when it comes to what resources they can afford to keep within their library collections. In order to make the most of one's budget, librarians need to understand what key questions, tools, and data they need to bring with them to the negotiating table. By being strategic while negotiating with vendors, the information professional can improve the value they receive for their budget dollars.

Preparing for the negotiation

Knowledge and tasks

- Connect with your users.
- Develop a list of questions to ask the vendor.

- Understand your library's content and the format in which it is delivered.

- If the resource is electronic, connect with your IT department to see what the technological limitations are.

- Have a good understanding of what you must walk away with and what you are willing to do without.

- Identify alternative products and vendors when possible to give you a better bargaining advantage at the table.

- Understand the digital content life cycle: discovery, trial, analysis, selection, acquisition, deployment, promotion, usage study, continuation, and alignment.

Questions to ask

- What is the level of interest amongst library users in this resource?

- If the product is fee-based, what is your budget?

- What are the expectations of your library's users?

- Is there a trial available and if so, how is use counted?

- How often has it been suggested as an addition by your users?

- Is there a state library consortium that can provide your library with discounts?

- Is the content you are seeking to add already delivered by other resources in your current collection?

- If there are multiple sources for this content, what is the best way to provide the content to your users?

- While the provider may give you a special deal for the first year, will you get a shocking renewal bill next year?

Negotiation

Knowledge and tasks

- Keep your trial statistics with you.
- Take your ego out of the equation.
- Have information about the product with you.
- Provide the final negotiated contract to your legal department for review.
- Have a copy of the license with you along with other communications sent between you and the vendor.
- Understand that when a cash discount is unavailable, the vendor may be open to providing you with non-monetary incentives to close the deal.

Questions to ask

- Are your print and digital subscriptions tied?
- If you choose to cancel the print subscription, will this affect your digital subscription?
- Must access to the content be bought as part of a package or can it be individually purchased?
- Is there an option to purchase resources as a bundled packaged to negotiate a volume discount?
- Is it possible to negotiate a multi-year agreement that will save you and the vendor time and money?
- Is the vendor willing to add a trial of a new product or other throw-ins when a cash discount is unavailable?
- For vendor protective clauses, are they willing to reword the clause so that protection is extended to both parties?

- Is the vendor willing to limit damages to the amount of the contract if your organization runs afoul (not deliberate)?
- Is the access/pricing model something that will work for your library and users? If not, is the vendor willing to work with you?
- Will the provider agree to supply perpetual access to content already subscribed to even if a decision is made to end the subscription in the future?

After the negotiation

Knowledge and tasks

- Study your usage.
- Create a podcast advertising the new addition.
- Create a screencast to educate users on how to use the resource.
- Promote the content via your Library 2.0 sites, library website, newsletters, and handouts at the desk.
- Cultivate the relationship with the vendor and stay in regular contact with them—not just for problem resolution.

Questions to ask

- How is use counted?
- Does the content have a high cost-per-use ratio?
- Were you successful in making the content cross the user's information-seeking path?
- If the usage has dropped but the fee has increased, how do you work with the provider in this case?

- How frequently did users experience problems accessing the content and how effectively did the provider respond?

- For subscription rate increases, ask the provider to explain how the increase will supply additional value to your users.

- Since you decided to acquire the content, have other options become available for delivering similar content to your users in a more effective or efficient way?

References

Chapter 1

Anderson, J. (1996) *Guide for Written Collection Policy Statements*. Chicago: American Library Association.

Anjejo, R. (2006) "Collection Development Policies for Small Libraries," *PNLA Quarterly*, 70(2), 12–16.

Bergman, B. and Laskowski, M. (2004) "Academic Media Center Collection Development and Circulation Policies: A Comparative Analysis," *College & University Media Review*, 10(2), 85–118.

Crosetto, A. (2011) "Weeding e-books," Booklist Online, available from: *http://www.booklistonline.com/Weeding-E-books-Alice-Crosetto/pid=5152179* (last accessed July 4, 2013).

Fombad, M. and Mutula, S. (2003) "Collection Development Practices at the University of Botswana Library (UBL)," *Malaysian Journal of Library and Information Science*, 8(1), 65–81.

Gray, C. and Metz, P. (2005) "Public Relations and Library Weeding," *Journal of Academic Librarianship*, 31(3), 273–9.

Hane, P.J. (2012) "A Librarian E-Book Revolution?" *Information Today*, 29(5), 10.

Hoffmann, F. and Wood, R. (2005) *Library Collection Development Policies*. Oxford: Scarecrow Press.

Johal, J. and Quigley, T. (2012) "Six Years of Floating Collections: The Vancouver Experience," *Public Libraries*, 51(3), 13–14.

Jones, C. (2007) "Maintaining a Healthy Library Collection: The Need to Weed," *Australasian Public Libraries and Information Services*, 20(4), 170–2.

Jones, D. (2006) "Oversized and Underused: Size Matters in Academic Libraries," *College and Research Libraries*, 67(4), 325–33.

Larson, J. (2008) *CREW: A Weeding Manual for Modern Libraries*. Austin, TX: Texas State Library and Archives.

Lean Enterprise Institute. (n.d.). "What is Lean," Available from: *http://www.lean.org/whatslean/*

Lilburn, J. (2003) "Re-examining the Concept of Neutrality for Academic Librarians," *Feliciter*, 49(1), 30–2.

Munroe, M., Haar, J.M., and Johnson, P. (2001) *Guide to Collection Development and Management Administration, Organization, and Staffing*. Lanham, MD: Scarecrow Press.

Phillips, L. (2013) "A List of Print-On-Demand and Self-Publishing 'Vanity Presses' for Librarians and Faculty," available from: *http://usp.ac.fj.libguides.com/pod* (accessed February 23, 2013).

Chapter 2

Cornell, J. (2012) *Lean Mean Circ Machine*. Presentation delivered at Michigan Library Association Annual Conference, November 7, 2012, Detroit, MI. Retrieved from *http://www.mla.lib.mi.us/node/1606* (last accessed June 27, 2013).

Lean Enterprise Institute. (n.d.) *What is lean?* Available from *http://www.lean.org/whatslean* (last accessed June 27, 2013).

Chapter 3

Creative Research Systems. (n.d.) *The Survey System Sample Size Calculator*. Available from *http://www.surveysystem. com/sscalc.htm* (last accessed July 4, 2013).

eHow (n.d.). *How to Calculate Sample Size Formula*. Available from *http://www.ehow.com/how_5262463_ calculate-sample-size-formula.html* (last accessed July 4, 2013).

Huber, J. (2011) *Lean Library Management: Eleven Strategies for Reducing Costs and Improving Customer Services*. New York: Neal-Schuman.

Urbaniak, G.C. and Plous, S. (n.d.) *Research Randomizer*. Available from *http://www.randomizer.org*.

U.S. Department of Health and Human Services. (n.d.) *Calculating Sample Size*. Retrieved from *http://bphc.hrsa. gov/policiesregulations/performancemeasures/ patientsurvey/calculating.html* (last accessed June 27, 2013).

Chapter 4

Retief, E. and Terblanche, F. (2006) "Role of Inventory Control in the Service Quality of an Academic Library in Regard to Library Material Access," *Mousaion Journal*, 24(1), 75–95.

Chapter 5

Library of Michigan. (n.d.) "Quality Services Audit Checklist." Available from *http://www.michigan.gov/*

*libraryofmichigan/0,2351,7-160-18668_45510---,00.
html* (last accessed July 4, 2013).

Library Research Service (n.d.) "Definition of Terms."
Available from *http://www.lrs.org/data-tools/public-
libraries/definition-of-terms* (last accessed July 4, 2013).

Chapter 6

Carter, B. (2007) "Leading Forward by Looking Backward,"
Library Media Connection, 23(4), 16–20.

Hartzell, G. (2002) "Controlling Your Own Destiny: Why
Vision and Mission Statements Are Indispensable," *School
Library Journal*, 48(11), 37.

Knievel, J., Wicht, H., and Silipigni Connaway, L. "Use of
Circulation Statistics and Interlibrary Loan Data in
Collection Management," *College and Research Libraries*,
67(1), 35–49.

Milwaukee Public Library. (n.d.) "Library Vision and
Mission Statements." Available from *http://www.mpl.org/
file/library_mission.htm* (last accessed July 4, 2013).

Chapter 7

Brisco, S. (2004) "Dewey or Dalton? An Investigation of
the Lure of the Bookstore," *Library Media Connection*,
22(4), 36–7.

Clark, R. (2008) "Impact Library Access with Bold Use of
Color and Space," *Library Media Connect*, 27(2), 16–18.

Fister, B. (2009) "Dewey Dilemma," *Library Journal*,
134(16), 22–5.

Fraser, M. and Munro, H. (2004). "A Good Fit: One Library's Experience with Ergonomic Design," *Public Libraries*, 43(4), 233–8.

Greiner, T. (2005) "Collection Development and Shelf Space: A Proposal for Nonfiction Collections," *Public Libraries*, 44(6), 347–50.

Hopkins, S. (2007) "Decimating Dewey: Introducing a Bookshop Arrangement for Shelving the Nonfiction Collection," *Australasian Public Libraries and Information Services*, 20(1), 8–13.

Ragsdale, K. and Kenney, D. (1995) "Spec Flyer 208: Effective Library Signage," available from *http://old.arl. org/bm~doc/spec-208-flyer.pdf* (last accessed July 4, 2012).

Schmidt, J. and Wilson, H. (1998) "Designing the Real Virtual Library: An Overview of the Preparation of An Upgrade for the University of Queensland Library," available from *http://bit.ly/12pNEoT* (last accessed July 4, 2013).

Chapter 8

Ashmore, B. and Grogg, J.E. (2009) "The Art of the Deal: Negotiation Advice from Library Leaders and Vendors," *Searcher*, 17(1), 18–25.

Duncan, S., Campbell, E., Rastogi, S., and Wilson, J. (1998) "Sources of Funding for Public Libraries," in Whitesides, W. (ed.) *Reinvention of the Public Library for the 21st Century*. Englewood, CO: Libraries Unlimited. Pp.150–79.

Hoffert, B. (2007) "Who's Selecting Now? As Phoenix Public Library Boldly Passes On Selection Responsibilities to Its Vendors, Some Libraries Follow—and Others Dig In," *Library Journal*, 132(14), 40–4.

Hogan, C. (2008) "Library Book Sales: Cleaning House or Cleaning Up?" *Searcher*, 16(3), 36–46.

Oder, N. (2009) "Adjustment Time: Libraries Are Either Tightening Budgets or Preparing to Do so," *Library Journal*, 134 (1), 32–4.

Stickell, L. and Nickel, L. (2011) "Grant Proposals for the Working Librarian: From Idea to Implementation," in C. Smallwood (ed.), *The Frugal Librarian: Thriving in Tough Economic Times*. Chicago: American Library Association.

Chapter 9

Asantewa, D. (2003) "Holistic Budgeting: A Process: A Whole System Approach," *Information Outlook*, 7(8), 14–18.

Berry, J.N. (2008) "The Impact Library: Laramie County Library System, WY," *Library Journal*, 133(11), 34–7.

Corlett, K. (2009) "Best Job Shadowing," *Inside Business*, 11(9), 17.

Leung, K. (2009, August 29). "Cross Training Has Long-Term Benefits HR Trends," *South China Morning Post*.

Nelson, S. (2009) *Implementing for Results: Your Strategic Plan in Action*. Chicago, American Library Association.

Nicholson, S. (2004) "Conceptual Framework for the Holistic Measurement and Cumulative Evaluation of Library Services," *Journal of Documentation*, 60(2), available from *http://bibliomining.com/nicholson/ nicholsonpdfs/holistic.pdf* (last accessed July 4, 2013).

Appendix B

Guevara, S. (2009) *"Strategic Content Negotiation for the Small Library,"* Poster Presentation, 2009 Michigan Library Association Annual Conference, Lansing, MI. Available from *http://www.slideshare.net/sophiaguevara/ 2009-michigan-library-association-conference-poster-presentation* (last accessed July 4, 2013).

Index